Law House,
Airdrie Road,
Carluke,
ML8 5ER

Institute of Leadership
& Management

superseries

Developing Yourself and Others

FIFTH EDITION

Published for the
Institute of Leadership & Management

ELSEVIER

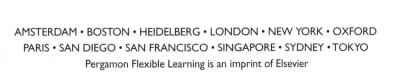

AMSTERDAM • BOSTON • HEIDELBERG • LONDON • NEW YORK • OXFORD
PARIS • SAN DIEGO • SAN FRANCISCO • SINGAPORE • SYDNEY • TOKYO
Pergamon Flexible Learning is an imprint of Elsevier

Pergamon
Flexible
Learning

Pergamon Flexible Learning is an imprint of Elsevier
Linacre House, Jordan Hill, Oxford OX2 8DP, UK
30 Corporate Drive, Suite 400, Burlington, MA 01803, USA

First edition 1986
Second edition 1991
Third edition 1997
Fourth edition 2003
Fifth edition 2007

Copyright © 1986, 1991, 1997, 2003, 2007 ILM. Published by Elsevier Ltd. All rights reserved

Editor: David Pardey

Based on material in previous editions of this work

The views expressed in this work are those of the authors and do
not necessarily reflect those of the Institute of Leadership &
Management or of the publisher

No part of this publication may be reproduced, stored in a retrieval system or transmitted in any
form or by any means electronic, mechanical, photocopying, recording or otherwise without the
prior written permission of the publisher

Permissions may be sought directly from Elsevier's Science & Technology Rights Department in
Oxford, UK: phone (+44) (0) 1865 843830; fax (+44) (0) 1865 853333; email: permissions@
elsevier.com. Alternatively you can submit your request online by visiting the Elsevier website at
http://elsevier.com/locate/permissions, and selecting Obtaining permission to use Elsevier material

Notice
No responsibility is assumed by the publisher for any injury and/or damage to persons or
property as a matter of products liability, negligence or otherwise, or from any use or operation
of any methods, products, instructions or ideas contained in the material herein

British Library Cataloguing in Publication Data
A catalogue record for this book is available from the British Library

Library of Congress Cataloguing in Publication Data
A catalogue record for this book is available from the Library of Congress

ISBN 978-0-08-046414-5

For information on all Pergamon Flexible Learning publications
visit our website at http://books.elsevier.com

Institute of Leadership & Management
Registered Office
1 Giltspur Street
London
EC1A 9DD
Telephone: 020 7294 2470
www.i-l-m.com
ILM is part of the City & Guilds Group

Typeset by Charon Tec Ltd (A Macmillan Company), Chennai, India
www.charontec.com
Printed and bound in Great Britain

07 08 09 10 11   10 9 8 7 6 5 4 3 2 1

Working together to grow
libraries in developing countries

www.elsevier.com | www.bookaid.org | www.sabre.org

ELSEVIER   BOOK AID International   Sabre Foundation

Contents

Contents

Reflect and review   127

Series preface

Whether you are a tutor/trainer or studying management development to further your career, Super Series provides an exciting and flexible resource to help you to achieve your goals. The fifth edition is completely new and up-to-date, and has been structured to perfectly match the Institute of Leadership & Management (ILM)'s new unit-based qualifications for first line managers. It also harmonizes with the 2004 national occupational standards in management and leadership, providing an invaluable resource for S/NVQs at Level 3 in Management.

Super Series is equally valuable for anyone tutoring or studying any management programmes at this level, whether leading to a qualification or not. Individual workbooks also support short programmes, which may be recognized by ILM as Endorsed or Development Awards, or provide the ideal way to undertake CPD activities.

For learners, coping with all the pressures of today's world, Super Series offers you the flexibility to study at your own pace to fit around your professional and other commitments. You don't need a PC or to attend classes at a specific time – choose when and where to study to suit yourself! And you will always have the complete workbook as a quick reference just when you need it.

For tutors/trainers, Super Series provides an invaluable guide to what needs to be covered, and in what depth. It also allows learners who miss occasional sessions to 'catch up' by dipping into the series.

Super Series provides unrivalled support for all those involved in first line management and supervision.

Unit specification

Title:	Developing yourself and others		Unit Ref:	M3.13
Level:	3			
Credit value:	2			

Learning outcomes	Assessment criteria	
The learner will	**The learner can (in an organization with which the learner is familiar)**	
1. Know how to identify development needs and develop self and others to achieve organizational objectives	1.1	Use at least *one* simple technique for identifying own development needs and the development needs of *one* other member of the team
	1.2	Identify own learning style(s) and the learning style(s) of *one* other member of the team
	1.3	Briefly analyse *two* learning/development options to meet need(s) of self and *one* other member of the team
	1.4	Identify barriers to learning and explain how these barriers can be overcome
	1.5	Identify support mechanisms for the development of self and *one* other member of the team
	1.6	Describe methods used to monitor the development of self and *one* other member of the team

Workbook introduction

1 ILM Super Series study links

This workbook addresses the issues of *Developing yourself and Others*. Should you wish to extend your study to other Super Series workbooks covering related or different subject areas, you will find a comprehensive list at the back of this book.

2 Links to ILM qualifications

This workbook relates to the learning outcomes of Unit M.3.13 Developing yourself and others from the ILM Level 3 Award, Certificate and Diploma in First Line Management.

3 Links to S/NVQs in management

This workbook relates to the following Units of the Management Standards which are used in S/NVQs in Management, as well as a range of other S/NVQs:

A2. Manage your own resources and professional development

D7. Provide learning opportunities for colleges

◉ 4 Workbook objectives

In all the other Super Series workbooks the emphasis is upon you acquiring knowledge and skills that will help you to be more effective in managing resources, change, quality, other people, information, and so on. In the first three sessions of this workbook the emphasis is on **you** as the person who has to acquire the knowledge and these skills and then put them to good use in your place of work. How well you can do this depends on how good you are at managing yourself.

In this workbook you will look at how you can identify and access development opportunities that will support you in becoming more effective in your job role. This requires you to understand not only what your job requires you to do, but also what skills, knowledge and personal attributes to do it. The workbook will encourage you to honestly assess how well you perform your managerial role, and the information you gather during this process will help you to identify your specific development needs. You will also be given the opportunity to fully evaluate and measure the value of the development opportunities available to you.

But, as a manager, you will almost certainly also have some responsibility for coaching and training your work team. You may be expected to organize different types of development activities, such as induction training for new employees, training in new tasks for individuals or introducing totally new skills to the work team. Occasionally you may also be called upon to carry out specific training such as safety training.

Skills development is a complicated process. The simplest way to approach it is to divide it into four stages:

Stage 1 – Assessing training needs
Stage 2 – Planning and preparation
Stage 3 – Delivering the training
Stage 4 – Giving feedback, evaluating the results and providing further support as necessary.

This workbook concentrates on the first and second stages, assessing training needs, and planning and preparation. The second two stages are discussed in another workbook in this series, *Coaching and Training Your Work Team*. When planning training you need to be able to identify training needs that would help both individuals and work teams meet work objectives. This requires you to collect and analyse information and present it to others for discussion or approval. Training needs analysis is discussed in Session D. In Session E you will learn how to plan training in an organized and scheduled manner and take into account all the resources that are available. This happens in a variety of ways in different workplaces. In some workplaces this is done in a very formal and structured way and in others it is more simple. However it is done, it is important that it is done well – the future of your work team and your workplace may depend upon it.

4.1 Objectives

When you have worked through this workbook you will be better able to:

- Analyse and build a sound picture of your current skills, knowledge and personal attributes, using a range of techniques and approaches.
- Undertake a personal training and development needs analysis.
- Develop and revise your own personal development plan.
- Identify and select appropriate training and development opportunities and any barriers to successful learning.
- Evaluate and record the training and development activities that you have been involved in.
- Use different techniques to collect and analyse information for training needs analysis purposes;
- Contribute to the identification of training and development needs for individuals and work teams;
- Set objectives for training and development;
- Contribute to planning training and development;
- Draw up a training plan.

5 Activity planner

The following activities require planning and some will take considerable time to complete so you may want to look at these now.

- Activity 2 on page 3 asks you to gather a range of information and detail your particular job role.
- Activities 6–8 on pages 7–14 take you through a comprehensive analysis your strengths and weaknesses.
- Activity 9 on page 16 asks you to complete a detailed PESTLE analysis, where you may need to consult experts to ensure your knowledge is up-to-date.
- Activity 12 on page 20 asks you to arrange with two people to discuss yourself assessment.

■ Activity 39 on page 84 asks you to analyse the skills needed to carry out a particular job.

■ Activity 41 on page 90 looks at versatility charts.

■ Activity 47 on page 104 is concerned with initial assessment plans.

■ Activity 54 on page 117 asks you to record a training plan.

Some or all of these Activities may provide the basis of evidence for your S/NVQ portfolio. Activities and the work-based assignment are signposted with this icon.

The icon states the elements to which the Portfolio Activities and Work-based assignment relate.

The Work-based assignment on page 124 is designed to help you meet Unit A2 Manage your own resources and professional development of the national occupational standards. You may want to prepare for it in advance.

Session A
Assessing your current situation

1 Introduction

This first session will allow you to explore the nature of your job and how you do it. We begin by asking you to examine some of the most basic aspects of it. Why does your job exist at all? What would happen (or not happen) if your job did not exist? We then take you step-by-step through an analysis of the requirements of your job. You'll re-examine your job description to see what you really are expected to do, and then look over the person specification and reflect on which of the skills and attributes listed there you already possess, and which ones you may feel you still need to acquire.

We then move on to look at how you can assess your own performance in your first line management role. What areas are you good at? Where do you think you need to reassess what you do? We introduce you to some common techniques to enable you to look at your areas of strength and weakness, and analyse where opportunities and threats might lie.

Having undertaken a detailed look at your own role and how you perform it, we encourage you to take the results of your analysis to others for their comment and feedback. In this way you'll develop an all-round and – more importantly – objective picture of how you're doing now. This process will enable you to see where you need to take action to develop your skills and knowledge. It will also demonstrate where your strengths are appreciated and where any opportunities for future career developments may be found.

You'll follow up what you find out in Session B, where we'll look at how you can begin to develop areas of weakness into strengths, and threats into opportunities.

2 Analysing the requirements of your job

Each and every job has a particular objective, a reason for its existence within the organization. Remove that job and something that is essential to the success of the organization cannot happen. The first activity asks you to think about why your own job exists.

Activity 1

5 mins

Why is your job necessary to the organization? What could **not** happen if your job did not exist?

_____

_____

_____

_____

Your answer will depend on precisely what your job is, but you may have linked it up to the jobs of other people, and specified how they depend on you to do what you do to get what they need to be done. For example, unless you issue weekly instructions to your team members, they may not know what they are supposed to be doing. Unless you give feedback to your line manager, he or she may not be able to make longer-term strategic plans.

Every job is made up of **key tasks and activities**. These are the different elements of the job that you perform in order to get the job done. In the examples given in the previous paragraph, two key tasks or activities were described – 'issue weekly instructions to team members' and 'give feedback to my line manager'.

In order to complete these key tasks and activities, the job holder should:

- possess **skills** relevant to the tasks and activities;
- hold **knowledge** that underpins, or supports these skills;
- possess certain **personal attributes** that are appropriate to the job.

For example, to successfully undertake the key tasks listed above, you would require good communication skills, you would need to know what your team had achieved, and know how to present that information in a suitable form to your line manager. You might also need the personal attributes of approach-ability and clear-headedness in order to find out that information and present it in a suitable manner.

The next activity gives you the opportunity to explore each of these aspects of your own job.

Activity 2

Gather documentation that will supply information on:

- your actual job role – its key tasks and activities;
- the skills, knowledge and behaviour essential to fulfilling these tasks and activities.

Make a brief list of the various documents that you have gathered.

_____

_____

_____

_____

_____

Job-related information comes in a range of forms and from a variety of sources. You might have obtained:

- a job description – that details the practicalities and requirements of the job;
- a person specification – that sets out the essential and desirable skills, knowledge and personal attributes needed by the job holder;
- completed appraisal or performance review forms – that contain information on how the person in the job is carrying out that job;
- an organization chart – showing the relationship between your job role and others within the company.

You might also have held discussions with your line manager, human resource staff, colleagues or others doing the same job as you to find out more.

2.1 The key tasks of your job

Activity 3

Using the information you have gathered, write down a list of the key tasks and activities that your job requires you to do.

_____

_____

_____

_____

_____

_____

Your answer to this activity will of course depend on the precise nature of your job. The point is that you are clear about what the key tasks actually are.

2.2 The skills, knowledge and personal attributes needed in your job

In order to be effective in doing our particular job, we need a combination of skills, knowledge and personal attributes. These need to support and complement one another. In the previous activity you listed the various tasks you do, all of which will require a different combination of skills, knowledge and personal attributes, in order for the person carrying out the work to be effective.

Activity 4

10 mins

Using the information you gathered in Activity 2, write down a list of the skills, knowledge and personal attributes that you need to possess to do your job.

_____

_____

_____

_____

Again, the answer you give will depend on the nature of your job, but you may have mentioned items as varied as good communication skills, a head for figures or a good memory, sensitivity in dealing with the public, or a disciplined approach to paperwork.

Up until now, we've asked you to look at the requirements of your job overall. Now let's look at what it needs in a bit more detail.

Activity 5

5 mins

Identify **one** key task of your current job, and write a brief description of it.

_____

_____

_____

Now ask yourself the following questions.

■ What do I need to be able to **do** to carry out this key part of my job (skill)?

_____

■ What do I need to **know** to carry out this key part of my job (knowledge)?

_____

■ What personal attributes do I need to **possess** to carry out this part of my job?

_____

There's no right answer here, since it will depend on which task you chose. If you had identified giving presentations as your example, then you might have identified the skill of preparing overhead slides, or handouts. The obvious knowledge in this instance would be the knowledge of the actual subject area, and knowledge of how to present information in a way that can be understood by your audience. The personal attributes might have included having the self-confidence to stand in front of the audience concerned.

Each task required by your job can be analysed in terms of the necessary skills, knowledge and personal attributes needed by the person doing it.

2.3 Assessing your own performance

Having looked at what your job requires, both in terms of its essential tasks and activities, and what it requires of you, we'll now go on to explore how good **you** feel you are at your job. How well do you think you perform on a day-to-day basis? Don't worry! The point about this exercise is not to make you feel that you're falling short in some way. Rather, it's to give you the chance to examine where your own development needs lie. This will not only help you to see how you might do your current job more effectively, but also give your confidence a boost and help you to see how your future career might develop. All managers, even the ones at the top of organizations, need to undertake this sort of assessment at one time or another, so you aren't being asked to do anything out of the ordinary here.

It has probably occurred to you that your own self-assessment may turn out to be a bit biased! In a later activity, we'll ask you to get other colleagues to give their opinion of the results. You might find it useful to begin thinking about who you might approach.

The one thing that's clear about managerial roles is that they are all different. So, how can we possibly go about assessing our performance? What activities do they all have in common that we can use as benchmarks? Although your job may be quite specific in terms of the practical activities you carry out, the role of any manager is likely to include managing:

- activities and quality;
- financial and physical resources;
- other people, yourself and relationships;
- communication and information.

The next activity is designed to help you begin to think about how well you do the tasks required in these four different aspects of your job.

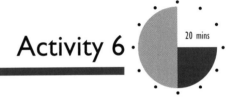

Activity 6

S/NVQ
A2

This Activity may provide the basis of appropriate evidence for your S/NVQ portfolio. If you are intending to take this course of action it might be better to write your answers on separate sheets of paper.

The following questionnaire will provide you with a preliminary picture of your own effectiveness across these areas of management. The tasks and activities illustrated are by no means a comprehensive listing of all the aspects of management in which you might be involved, but are meant to offer you the opportunity to consider these fundamental areas of your work.

(You may want to look back at the list of key tasks you drew up in Activity 3, to see whether it includes any essential tasks not contained in the questionnaire. If it does, add them to the questionnaire in the spaces provided.)

For each checklist item, ask yourself to what extent you usually achieve either the effects you intended or the outcomes that others (your manager, staff, customers, etc.) expect from you. Give yourself a rating from 1 to 5, where 1 equals 'very poor' and 5 equals 'very good', by circling the appropriate number in the column headed 'How effective are you?'.

Be as honest as you can. However, if you have sufficient time to consult someone else, then you might want to include their input as well. The results of this questionnaire are for your benefit only, and will give a basis for consideration later in this session.

a   Manage activities and quality

Tasks/Activities	How effective are you?
Agree requirements with internal and/or external customers.	1 – 2 – 3 – 4 – 5
Explain customer requirements to team members and to others both within and outside the organization.	1 – 2 – 3 – 4 – 5
Plan work activities to meet required objectives.	1 – 2 – 3 – 4 – 5
Identify areas where quality can be improved.	1 – 2 – 3 – 4 – 5
Involve others in making improvements to work activities.	1 – 2 – 3 – 4 – 5
Implement and co-ordinate planned change.	1 – 2 – 3 – 4 – 5
Assess the costs (either increases or savings) associated with change.	1 – 2 – 3 – 4 – 5
Monitor the team's work.	1 – 2 – 3 – 4 – 5
Inform others of their legal and organizational responsibilities in terms of health and safety.	1 – 2 – 3 – 4 – 5
Ensure that working conditions conform to legal and organizational requirements for health, safety and the environment.	1 – 2 – 3 – 4 – 5
	1 – 2 – 3 – 4 – 5

b   Manage financial and physical resources

Tasks/Activities	How effective are you?
Measure your team's performance against agreed objectives.	1 – 2 – 3 – 4 – 5
Monitor performance against budget, and reduce unacceptable variances.	1 – 2 – 3 – 4 – 5
Maintain an effective system for supply, storage and issue of materials for operations.	1 – 2 – 3 – 4 – 5
Plan the activities of team members to achieve work objectives.	1 – 2 – 3 – 4 – 5
Monitor the use of resources.	1 – 2 – 3 – 4 – 5
Identify staffing needs.	1 – 2 – 3 – 4 – 5
Control the use of equipment and maintain it safely, efficiently and effectively.	1 – 2 – 3 – 4 – 5
Ensure the security of personnel, stock, equipment and data in the workplace.	1 – 2 – 3 – 4 – 5
Create and implement action plans to identify and reduce waste.	1 – 2 – 3 – 4 – 5
Maintain complete and accurate records of resource use.	1 – 2 – 3 – 4 – 5
	1 – 2 – 3 – 4 – 5

c   Manage other people, yourself and relationships

Tasks/Activities	How effective are you?
Assess both your own skills and those of your team members to identify development needs.	1 – 2 – 3 – 4 – 5
Create and implement development plans that contain specific, measurable and realistic objectives.	1 – 2 – 3 – 4 – 5
Organize training activities that are consistent with your team development plans.	1 – 2 – 3 – 4 – 5
Build an effective and mutually supportive team.	1 – 2 – 3 – 4 – 5
Recognize symptoms of stress in yourself and your team members, and resolve it effectively.	1 – 2 – 3 – 4 – 5
Manage your team in accordance with the principles of equal opportunity and diversity.	1 – 2 – 3 – 4 – 5
Identify and implement appropriate solutions to problems.	1 – 2 – 3 – 4 – 5
Provide appropriate opportunities for team members to discuss problems.	1 – 2 – 3 – 4 – 5
Use motivation to ensure your team's commitment to change.	1 – 2 – 3 – 4 – 5
Manage time to meet your objectives.	1 – 2 – 3 – 4 – 5
	1 – 2 – 3 – 4 – 5

d   Manage communication and information

Tasks/Activities	How effective are you?
Gather accurate, sufficient and relevant information that is fit for its intended purpose.	1 – 2 – 3 – 4 – 5
Record and store information in ways that are in line with organizational systems and procedures.	1 – 2 – 3 – 4 – 5
Present information at a time and place, and in a form and manner appropriate to the intended recipients.	1 – 2 – 3 – 4 – 5
Obtain and give feedback, and use it to enhance performance.	1 – 2 – 3 – 4 – 5
Lead meetings in a way that helps people to make useful contributions, and which discourages unhelpful arguments and digressions.	1 – 2 – 3 – 4 – 5
Gain the trust and support of your line manager, colleagues and team members.	1 – 2 – 3 – 4 – 5
Collect verbal and non-verbal data and use it to interpret and monitor the attitudes of others.	1 – 2 – 3 – 4 – 5
Use networking as a tool to manage more effectively.	1 – 2 – 3 – 4 – 5
Use negotiation to resolve conflict.	1 – 2 – 3 – 4 – 5
Keep accurate, confidential records of conflicts and their outcomes.	1 – 2 – 3 – 4 – 5
	1 – 2 – 3 – 4 – 5

When you have completed the questionnaire, work out your average rating for each of the four areas of management. Do this by adding up the scores of all the relevant activities that you circled and divide by the number of relevant activities in that area. (For example, if you only circled four of the activities in 'Manage activities and quality', then add those scores together and divide by four.)

Put your four averages in the table below.

Managing activities and quality:	Managing financial and physical resources:
Managing other people, yourself and relationships:	Managing communication and information:

The results you obtain will show you which management areas you are good at, and which are likely ones for further development. For example, you might find that you scored a high average for managing resources, but less highly on managing people.

Activity 7 · 10 mins

S/NVQ A2

This Activity may provide the basis of appropriate evidence for your S/NVQ portfolio. If you are intending to take this course of action it might be better to write your answers on separate sheets of paper.

Look back at Activity 6 and, for each area of management activity, make a list of the skills or tasks in which you are particularly strong. Ask yourself these questions. What are my strengths? What am I good at? Where do I get positive results?

Managing activities and quality

_____

_____

_____

_____

_____

Managing financial and physical resources

_____
_____
_____
_____
_____

Managing other people, yourself and relationships

_____
_____
_____
_____
_____

Managing communication and information

_____
_____
_____
_____
_____

You may have found that, on consideration, you have certain strengths which you always took for granted. You may also have found that, on reflection, you are not as strong as you thought you were.

Activity 8 · 10 mins

S/NVQ A2

This Activity may provide the basis of appropriate evidence for your S/NVQ portfolio. If you are intending to take this course of action it might be better to write your answers on separate sheets of paper.

Now consider those areas in Activity 6 in which you consider yourself particularly weak. Again, list them according to management area, but this time give your reason (perhaps an example) to show why you think you are weak.

Area of weakness	My reason for thinking I am weak in this area is . . .
Managing activities and quality	
Managing financial and physical resources	
Managing other people, yourself and relationships	
Managing communication and information	

You should now have a comprehensive listing of all your main areas of strength and weakness. This will form the basis of much of your work in the rest of the workbook.

2.4 PESTLE analysis

A PESTLE analysis is a further approach that you can use to gauge your current and future effectiveness. You need to consider a variety of factors that will affect you and your organization. These factors are as follows.

- **P**olitical
- **E**conomic
- **S**ocial

- **T**echnological
- **L**egal
- **E**nvironmental/ecological

Political factors

The government affects the ways in which a business can operate, usually through the legal and regulatory controls that it applies. In the twenty-first century businesses need to face a range of political issues, for example relationships with overseas markets, development of transport systems, and world security issues.

Economic factors

Availability of money through an increased number of customers, or increased costs from suppliers will directly affect the business. At the same time changes to interest rates and inflationary effects will also have an impact upon how the business operates. Rates of exchange will also affect businesses that have dealings with customers or suppliers outside the UK. Stock market values may be another crucial factor.

Social factors

Organizations are affected by the availability of skilled and qualified staff, as well as the age and gender of the population from which it draws its staff. Issues such as child-care, or the care of elderly parents will affect working practices. Changing spending patterns and overall attitudes to careers will also have an impact on how the business operates and makes decisions.

Technological factors

As complex technology becomes more accessible, the methods and speed of communication will develop. Organizations can process and exchange information quickly, both within the business and in relation to its customers and suppliers. Organizations may face the need to keep its machinery up-to-date in order to compete, and so need to invest in new technologies on a regular basis.

Legal factors

There is legislation in place to cover, for example, accounting practices, trading practices, employment practices, waste disposal and processing. Existing legislation is not written in stone, and may be amended from time to time. In addition, new legislation is introduced frequently and so every business needs to be aware of the impact of legislation, existing and new, on its business practices.

Environmental/ecological factors

Organizations usually become aware of environmental factors when legislation is enacted, for example, to reduce carbon and sulphur emissions. There are costs associated with the management of such issues, but at the same time a business may wish to emphasize or develop its environmental 'persona' in order to increase its customer-base, where customer expectation is increased in this area.

Activity 9 · 25 mins

S/NVQ
A2

This Activity may provide the basis of appropriate evidence for your S/NVQ portfolio. If you are intending to take this course of action it might be better to write your answers on separate sheets of paper.

Complete the following chart, noting down those factors that might affect your organization, and you personally and as a manager, over the next three years. You may have to do some research to make sure that your own knowledge is up-to-date. Health and safety officers, personnel or human resource staff, for example, are likely sources of relevant information, in relation to legislative changes.

For example, if your organization needs to invest in new technology to remain competitive, you may be faced with the issue of staff redundancies, a potentially fraught and painful matter. Or, if new environmental legislation is introduced, you may find that your working practices have to change radically to take this into account – indeed, your job may change completely or even disappear.

FACTORS	ORGANIZATIONAL IMPACT	PERSONAL IMPACT
POLITICAL		
ECONOMIC		
SOCIAL		
TECHNOLOGICAL		
LEGAL		
ENVIRONMENTAL/ ECOLOGICAL		

Activity 10

Reflect upon your findings in Activity 9. Consider each of the factors that you have identified as having an impact upon you as a manager. Now ask yourself this question.

■ Will I be able to deal with these factors using my existing strengths?

Where the answer is 'NO' place an asterisk (*) next to the factor concerned.

3 Confirming your findings

The analyses that you have completed have provided you with a detailed range of information. You should now have a clear sense of your areas of strength and weakness, the areas where you are posed with both opportunities and threats, and where external factors will (or are likely to) affect your future capability.

However, what you have at present is just your own personal assessment. It is important that you confirm your findings by checking them with other people to see whether or not they agree with you.

Activity 11

S/NVQ A2

This Activity may provide the basis of appropriate evidence for your S/NVQ portfolio. If you are intending to take this course of action it might be better to write your answers on separate sheets of paper.

Complete the left-hand column of the following chart, inserting the relevant detail from your analysis (Activity 8) and the asterisked items from your PES-TLE analysis (Activity 9). Leave the commentator's name and job title box blank (the commentator can fill in those details for themselves).

Feedback on personal assessment of current effectiveness

Your name_____   Your job title_____

Commentator's name: _____ Commentator's job title: _____	Findings confirmed? Y/N	Commentator's feedback
My areas of current weakness.		
My potential areas for future development (threats).		
External factors that will require me to develop my existing skills and knowledge.		
This space is for the commentator to add detail on other areas of weakness/development that I should consider.		

Having filled in details of your personal assessment in the left-hand column of the chart, photocopy it at least twice. In the next activity you will give a copy to others for their comment and feedback.

3.1 Seeking feedback

Throughout our working lives, and as an integral part of development, we need to seek and receive constructive feedback. Feedback is essential, especially in the early stages of assessing our development needs, because we often see ourselves in a very different way to how others see us. Where we present others with our personal view we can ask them to confirm our own perceptions, and request their suggestions about possible ways forward. This can help to ensure that any development activity you decide to undertake is truly relevant.

To make sure that you get feedback that is constructive you need to do the following.

- Be specific; make it clear **what** you want the feedback on, and say **why** you want it – in this case to support you in becoming more effective.
- Ask for comments on particular areas of weakness. For example, if you say you are weak in asking questions, ask them to either agree or disagree, but ask that they also back this up with an example.
- Set the feedback in context; in this case you are asking for the feedback to help you to find out where you need to think more about personal or professional development.
- Check that you understand what has been offered as feedback. This is easy enough if you ask for verbal feedback, because you can clarify any ambiguities at the time. But where you seek written feedback (using the information from Activity 12 for example), follow this up quickly with a brief discussion. This is important in order to avoid any misunderstanding about what has been written.

For feedback to be valid and useful it should come from a range of different sources. Try and make sure that those offering the feedback are:

- in a position to offer feedback and comment, i.e. someone who works with you/for you or sees you performing your job;
- likely to be honest and constructive, and not just say what they think you might want to hear!

Activity 12

S/NVQ
A2

This Activity may provide the basis of appropriate evidence for your S/NVQ portfolio. If you are intending to take this course of action it might be better to write your answers on separate sheets of paper.

Give a completed copy of the chart from Activity 11 to at least two people. This might include your line manager, a member of your team and/or a work colleague. Arrange a suitable time with each person separately, to discuss their comments. You should make notes of what they say.

3.2 Completing the picture

Once you have received and checked the feedback from your colleagues about your self-assessment, you will then need to go over it again and summarize the main points of agreement about the areas of weakness that you have identified. This will give you your starting point for the next stage of this workbook – putting your development needs in order of priority, and specifying how you could go about meeting them.

Activity 13

Using the material you have gathered when discussing your self-assessment with your colleagues, write down a complete list of all the areas you have identified and agreed as needing some developmental input. Don't worry about priorities at this point, we'll look at that later in the next session.

_____

_____

_____

_____

_____

_____

Self-assessment 1

For questions 1 to 4 complete the sentences with a suitable word or words from the following list.

STORAGE	KNOWLEDGE	PEOPLE	SHOULD
SOURCES	TASKS	SKILLS	WEAKNESSES
STRENGTHS	MUST		

1   Job-related information comes in a range of forms and from a variety of
     _____.

2   Every job is made up of key _____ and activities.

3   In order to be effective we need a combination of skills, _____
     and personal attributes.

4   Weaknesses that _____ be addressed quickly are those that will
     involve job requirements that are fundamental to the overall day-to-day per-
     formance of your job.

5   What are the factors that comprise a PESTLE analysis?

     _____

     _____

     _____

     _____

     _____

     _____

6   Why is seeking feedback essential?

     _____

     _____

7   How can we make sure that feedback is valid and reliable?

     _____

     _____

     _____

Answers to these questions can be found on page 134.

4 Summary

- To become more effective we all need a starting point. We need to know what our present job requires of us and where we might be falling short. Even top managers need to reassess their performance once in a while, so this is a normal part of the development process.

- Every job is made up of key tasks and activities, and in order to complete these key tasks and activities, the jobholder should:

  - possess skills relevant to the tasks and activities;
  - hold knowledge that underpins, or supports these skills;
  - be able to behave appropriately within the environment of the job.

- Overall the role of a manager is likely to include managing:

  - activities and quality;
  - other people, yourself and relationships;
  - financial and physical resources;
  - communication and information.

- Throughout our working lives, and as an integral part of development, we need to seek and receive constructive feedback. Feedback is essential, particularly at the early stages of self-assessment, because we often see ourselves in a very different way to how others see us.

Session B
Choosing development activities that suit your needs

1 Introduction

Having completed the activities in Session A, you should by now have a clear picture of the personal and professional developmental issues you face as a manager. You may also have been pleasantly surprised by some of your colleagues' comments.

This session begins by looking at what 'development' means, and how it differs from two similar terms – training and learning. The session then builds on the work you did in Session A. First we will look at a simple procedure for enabling you to put your various development needs into a logical order. Then we look at how you can begin to convert your weaknesses into strengths by the process of setting yourself workable **performance objectives.**

The main part of the session looks at the relationship between the various development activities available to you, and your own process of learning, known as your **preferred learning style**. By having a clear understanding of the relationship between them, you will be better able to find a focus in the quite complex area of personal and professional development activity.

When looking at possible **forms of development activity**, you need to take two things into account before making your decision. There's the type of activity itself (we describe the most important of these first), and then there's the question of which of these are actually available to you in practice.

Every individual is different and no single development activity will suit everyone. However, most of us benefit from taking different approaches to learning, and it's crucial not to dismiss activities that don't seem to suit you at first glance, because by doing so you may miss useful opportunities.

By the end of this session, you should have a clear picture of which forms of development activity are available to you. You should also have a better idea of how your own learning process either fits with those activities, or where it might be at odds with them and how you might deal with this.

You'll then be equipped to move on to Session C, where you look at the practicalities of preparing a personal development plan.

2 What is 'development'?

There are whole books on the subject of development, and it's not the aim of this workbook to bog you down in the discussion of definitions! Having said that, a definition of some sort is necessary. So far, we've been using the term 'development' without really making it clear what we mean by it.

There is a tendency to confuse 'development' with 'training' and 'learning'. In fact, they refer to different things, and it's important to be clear about the differences. We'll briefly discuss training and learning first, in order to get a more precise idea of what 'development' means.

Training

Training is perhaps the most straightforward term. Training is a planned series of activities that enable the trainees to do something they couldn't do before. An expert demonstrates how to do something, and provides guidance to the trainees. For example, a gardener can be trained to use a chain-saw, a receptionist can be trained to use a switchboard or a graphic designer to use QuarkXpress. Training is usually linked to limited objectives, where we will be able to do something, or will know something, that we could not do or did not know before we were trained. The success of a training programme will depend mainly on how well it is organized and on the skill of the trainer.

Learning

Learning is perhaps most usefully defined as absorbing new information in such a way that we can apply it in practice. We learn in all sorts of different ways in the course of our lives – we learn how to talk and walk, we learn how to cook or write an essay, we learn how to play football and get on with other people. These examples involve very different processes, but all of them depend partly on our individual capabilities. Some people become master chefs, others can't even learn to boil an egg. Some people become award-winning writers, others avoid putting pen to paper again once they leave school. Learning therefore depends largely on our individual aptitude.

In summary then, we might describe the difference between training and learning as follows.

■ Training is the input of information from outside.
■ Learning is the internal process of absorbing and understanding that information so that we can put it into practice.

If you want to know more about training and learning, you can study *Coaching and Training Your Work Team* in this series.

Training and learning are both aspects of **development.**

Activity 14 · 2 mins

Write down your own brief definition of the word 'development'.

_____

_____

When we ask different people what they understand by this word we get a range of responses, including:

■ '… getting better at my job';
■ '… changing what we do for the better';
■ '… making the most of what I can already do';
■ '… taking different approaches to the way I do things';
■ '… going beyond what I can do now'.

Your definition may be different, but it probably contained a strong sense of movement and change.

Development

We can think of development as adding to something that is already there – a process of growth, of building on an existing foundation. Development is about personal and professional evolution and advancement; becoming better equipped to deal with the changes that affect us now and in the future. While development involves both training and learning it is more than the two of them put together. It also involves other, more personal factors, which are not easily defined.

You have probably already thought about the fact that completing this workbook is itself a professional development activity.

Activity 15 · 5 mins

Think about this workbook. Take a few minutes now to look through it, noting the various features it contains.

■ How does this workbook become part of your training? What features of the workbook meet the definition of training we gave earlier in this section?

_____

_____

■ How will you be able to demonstrate the learning that you may acquire from completion of this workbook?

_____

_____

■ Briefly summarize how you think that completion of this workbook will contribute to your development.

_____

_____

There are no correct answers to this activity, since they will depend on the nature of your job, but we can give general indications.

■ The workbook has clear objectives, as set out on page xiii, and can therefore be seen as a form of training. In addition, it has been produced by people who are expert in the field of development.

■ You will be able to demonstrate any learning acquired from this workbook by applying it to your role as a manager.

■ Completing the workbook will enable you to grow and advance in your ability to do your job, and perhaps consider new career moves.

3 Your development needs – in order of priority

You have examined the skills, knowledge and personal attribute requirements needed in your current job, analysed your areas of strength and weakness and sought feedback on your findings. The next stage is to begin prioritizing your actual development needs: in what order do you need to tackle them?

A simple approach is to ask yourself the following questions.

■ Are there any weaknesses that MUST be addressed quickly? These will be those that affect your day-to-day performance of your job.

■ Which weaknesses SHOULD be addressed over the next 3–6 months? (i.e. where you're only involved in the activity on an irregular basis, for example appraisal interviews.)

■ Which weaknesses COULD be addressed on a longer-term basis? For example, weaknesses that are less concerned with your current job than with your career aspirations.

Activity 16

Look at your list of identified and agreed weaknesses, which you drew up at the end of Session A. Put these weaknesses in order of priority, using the three questions above. Those weaknesses that MUST be addressed urgently should be labelled as 1, those that SHOULD be addressed within the medium term as 2, and finally those that COULD be addressed in the long term as 3.

Of course, if you have only identified one development need, the choice is simple, but you still need to be clear about what sort of need it is, and which of these three priorities it is.

_____

_____

_____

_____

_____

_____

Next to each development need you have listed here, note whether it is a skill, knowledge or a personal attribute that you need to acquire or develop.

This activity should have given you a sharper focus on your immediate development needs. We now move on to see how they can be turned into strengths by creating practical performance objectives.

4 Specifying your objectives

To change a weakness into a strength, you need to set yourself precise objectives that will work in practice. These can be used to measure your performance, so that you can tell when the weakness has become a strength.

For example, you may have identified an area of weakness such as 'I'm not up-to-date with the legislation about X.' Your objective might then be stated as 'To become familiar with the new legislation about X, and be able to explain it to the members of my team.'

Let's look at how we do this in a bit more detail.

Activity 17

5 mins

Maddi manages a team of eight researchers in a company that carries out market research by telephone and records the details on a database, for different companies across the UK. The team usually works in smaller groups for particular clients. The research projects change regularly, so Maddi has to brief her team on a weekly basis, allocating clients to the various smaller groups.

She has found out that she does not do this very effectively. Her team does not absorb the information that she gives them. Sometimes the team members are not sure who their clients for the week are, and this results in confusion. Essential tasks are not carried out by the right people, or are not carried out at all.

After several complaints, Maddi has realized that her weakness lies in how she gives out information, which does not enable her staff to carry out their work in a way that meets customer requirements. She has also realized that this weakness is a priority that must be addressed, because it is a task that she carries out on a weekly basis.

What does Maddi need to do that she is not doing now?

_____

_____

_____

One of the things you may have stated is that, during the weekly briefings, Maddi needs to give out information to all members of the team in a way that enables them to do their job, on a week-by-week basis.

What we have done is produce a 'statement of need', also called a **performance objective**. The performance objective changes a weakness into a positive statement of something that needs to be done. In other words, once Maddi is able to perform as stated, the weakness will have been addressed.

But we still don't know how this will be done. The objective is couched in very general terms. How do we bring it down to a practical level? Let's look at the different qualities a performance objective needs to have if it is to be of any immediate value.

In summary, objectives need to SMART. This means that an objective should be:

- **S**pecific
- **M**easurable
- **A**chievable
- **R**elevant
- **T**ime bound.

Specific

Specific means that the objective should state what actions need to be carried out, using language that is easily understood by everyone concerned. '*Conduct weekly briefings, giving out information to all members of the team*' is a specific statement of Maddi's task.

Measurable

For an objective to be **measurable** it needs to be set in a way that it can be assessed. If there is no measurement attached to the objective, such as '*... in a way that enables them to do their job, on a week-by-week basis*', it will be difficult to decide when it has been achieved, whether there has been a shortfall or where requirements have been exceeded. If each member of the team cannot explain what is required of him or her at the end of each briefing, and if the work is not carried out as stated, then Maddi has not achieved her performance objective.

Achievable

If an objective is to be **achievable**, it must take into account the resources available – including the resource of time. Maddi needs to set aside a particular amount of time per week for this briefing and allow herself sufficient preparation time – this might mean producing short briefings beforehand, in writing, for the different groups. To ensure that this objective is achievable, Maddi may need to review how her time is allocated across the rest of the week. The objective also needs to take into account the capabilities of the individual. For example, if Maddi's problem is not lack of time, but the skill needed to write a clear brief, she may need extra help with this.

Relevant

For an objective to be **relevant** it needs to make sense to the individual in terms of their job role, and to support the overall objectives of the department and the business. Maddi's overall responsibility is for the performance of her team, and these briefings are an essential part of this responsibility – hence this objective is clearly relevant to Maddi.

Time bound

Finally objectives need to be **time bound**. Questions to consider include the following.

■ When must the objective be achieved by?
■ When will the objective be reviewed?

Given that it is a regular part of her job, Maddi's objective is a high priority, so the objective needs to be achieved within the next month or two, at the very most.

Reviewing objectives is essential, in order to monitor your progress. If the objective needs to be achieved in, say, three months time, then the reviews should be carried out at least once a month. The person who carries out this review is likely to be the person with whom the objective was agreed, for example your line manager.

In the next session we will discuss how to review your performance objectives.

Activity 18 · 10 mins

Return to Activity 16 and take **two** of the areas of weakness that you have listed as priority 1.

_____

_____

Now convert these weaknesses into SMART performance objectives, i.e. **state what you will be able to do** when you have addressed these weaknesses, and they have been converted into strengths. As you do this, look back at the list of qualities that a SMART objective needs to have, to remind yourself of what each of those qualities involves.

_____

_____

_____

_____

_____

_____

Once you have undertaken a relevant development activity, you should be able to fulfil the performance objective.

5 Forms of development activity

Development activities take a variety of forms. Because personal and professional development is a different experience for each of us, it is important to recognize that there is such a variety of possibilities.

Activity 19

List all the different types, or forms, of development activity that you can think of.

_____

_____

_____

_____

_____

_____

You may have listed some or all of the following.

- Training courses and programmes.
- Coaching.
- Mentoring.
- Distance learning – using workbooks, possibly with tutor support, or through computer-based learning programmes accessible on-line.
- Work-based projects.
- E-learning, using computer-based training.
- Planned or guided reading.

We will now look at these forms of development and explore what is involved in each. One important clue to the type of activity you might consider as you read the descriptions that follow, is whether it's likely to be something you will enjoy. Your enjoyment of it will depend upon your preferred learning style, which we've mentioned before and will come back to later in this session.

5.1 Training courses and programmes

As we said earlier, these usually involve learning new skills, knowledge or ways of working. Training courses and programmes should have clearly stated objectives or learning outcomes, so that the participants know what to expect and can gauge the effectiveness of the training once it's completed. Look at the objectives before you start a training course, because this will help you and your line manager focus on what the training provides before you actually attend.

Training courses will be delivered through a variety of approaches. These approaches are designed to suit the learning styles of the different participants and keep the trainees interested, so a training programme will involve more than one training method. For example, demonstrations, presentations and discussions may all be used.

Advantages of training courses and programmes are:

- there is an exchange of ideas between the participants;
- teaching by experts in the subject;
- focus on particular skills, knowledge or personal attributes;
- the needs of a number of people are met in a cost effective way.

Disadvantages might include that:

- the costs can be high in some cases;
- the content may not be equally relevant to all participants;
- attendance may require time away from work.

5.2 Coaching

This is a one-to-one activity. Coaching is a process where an individual is actively supported in solving a problem or performing a task more effectively. For example, the first line manager may coach a team member in how to allocate tasks to other members of the workforce, or how to write reports. Or one team member may need to coach another in an aspect of their job when work processes or procedures change.

Coaching can provide excellent opportunities for development within the workplace, using existing resources and expertise.

Advantages of coaching are:

- the team or department has more than one person who can fill a particular role or function if necessary;
- the person being coached does not have to leave work in order to develop their skills;
- the skills and experience are immediately relevant to the job;
- it makes the job more interesting;
- both people involved are working with someone they know;
- it is a very cost-effective form of development.

Disadvantages are that:

- it can be very time consuming;
- singling out one individual in this way may cause resentment among other members of the workforce;
- the person who receives coaching may be encouraged to challenge the coach's authority;
- the coach may pass on poor working habits or practices;
- the coach may not be very good in this role, even if they are good at their job.

5.3 Mentoring

The mentor is an experienced person who helps the individual they are mentoring to clarify their professional goals. The mentor can discuss with the mentee what they want to achieve and how they can best go about attaining this (e.g. by acquiring certain skills and/or experience). They then act as a means of support and guidance as the mentee goes about achieving their goals over a period of time. At the end of the mentoring process the mentor and mentee review the process and review the goals if necessary.

A mentor is likely to be someone with experience of an organization, a job, or a particular way of working. In many cases, a mentor can help an individual to access resources (such as information or professional contacts) that were previously unknown to them or out of their reach. Usually, the mentor is not someone in authority with whom the individual works directly (such as their line manager), since mentoring is more like an informal partnership than an authority relationship.

The advantages and disadvantages are similar to those of coaching, although because the mentoring relationship does not overlap with work roles, the person being mentored is not singled out from their colleagues in the same way.

5.4 Distance learning

Distance learning enables individuals to undertake development opportunities and approaches to learning in their own time and at their own pace, and without having to attend formal courses. It's also called 'flexible' or 'open' learning. Distance learning can include:

■ written open learning workbooks and packs, like this one;
■ audio visual learning – through tapes, CDs, television programmes, videos, DVDs;
■ e-learning by way of CD-ROM training packages, on-line training or on-line conferencing.

For distance learning to be effective it is important that individuals are given adequate support. This might mean that individuals on distance/flexible learning programmes have regular access to a tutor, or to fellow learners at workshops. Programmes of distance learning can be cost-effective, and flexible as they can be adapted to suit individual needs and circumstances.

Its **advantages** are that it is flexible, the learner progresses at the pace most suitable to him or her, and it is usually less expensive than an attendance course. **Disadvantages** include the fact that students may work almost entirely alone, which can make motivation difficult.

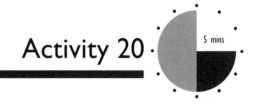

Activity 20 · 5 mins

Write down what you personally have found to be the advantages and disadvantages of learning by this method when using this workbook.

_____

_____

_____

_____

_____

5.5 Work-based projects

Designing work-based projects linked to your performance objectives is a worthwhile and practical approach. Such projects can be cost-effective and cost-efficient, because they will make use of existing resources, and may in fact be designed to maximize the use of these resources. Development becomes part and parcel of work, as individuals will be expected to stretch themselves, applying their skills and knowledge in new ways. Work-based projects can also help with transferability of skills and knowledge, especially where they meet both the needs of the learner and those of the organization.

> Helena had recently begun working as the first line manager for an office administration team. When she started the job, Helena's line manager talked through the current situation and highlighted the fact that recent computerization had caused a number of problems.
>
> Helena and her manager had agreed that – as part of her development, and in order to be able to assure the quality of the records (a key part of her job) – she would carry out a thorough analysis of the current situation. She would hold individual discussions with all team members and draw up a recommended plan of action, including suggestions for training and development. She would hold a one hour weekly meeting with her line manager to review progress, and check that she was working along the right lines.

This example summarizes an approach to work-based projects that is practical and relevant to the individual's performance at work. Helena is developing her skills, knowledge and personal attributes while solving a problem in a real work situation, which is both cost and time efficient and effective.

It can be tempting to see work-based projects as being always the best way to develop at work, because they focus on the work at hand. However, such projects must be carefully thought out. They must be linked closely to the learner's performance objective(s) as well as to organizational needs, so that the learner feels that the experience was useful and relevant. Where you wish to use this form of development, you need to be sure that you will receive solid support and guidance. It may be most effectively used along with coaching or mentoring (see above).

5.6 E-learning

As we become more information-technology literate, computer-based training is becoming more widespread. It can take the form of CD-ROM material that takes the learner through different scenarios, asking you to make choices, or where you interact with the package and learn through the decisions that you take. These programs may include text, images, and also audio or video material.

This form of development depends upon the computer resources available. Such programs may also be available through the Internet. It is likely that in the future, 'online' and 'distance' learning will come to mean the same thing.

The **advantages** of e-learning are:

- development can usually be done in modular form, so the learner can pick and choose what they need from a range of modules;
- the learners go at their own pace, and can repeat their studies as often as they like until they feel proficient;
- it is relatively cheap.

Its **disadvantages** are that:

- the isolation does not suit some people;
- not everyone is happy working with a machine;
- it is not always suitable if the topic you want to study is developing rapidly, since the material will date quickly.

5.7 Planned or guided reading

Planned or guided reading is a form of development that enables you to expand your knowledge in a particular field or area. Sources will include:

- the Internet;
- professional journals and publications;
- books;
- specialist sections of newspapers.

As mentioned above, the Internet is a vast source of information about every imaginable subject. Because the array of sources is so wide (and of varying quality), your reading needs to be planned or guided by someone who knows the field. You will need to focus on the area of knowledge that will enable you to fulfil your agreed performance objective.

One obvious source of access to books and journals is your local library. Even if its own stock is quite limited, it can supply you with books or journals from other libraries, using centralized ordering systems. You may come across a journal that contains regular and relevant information, either in relation to your current role or to your future career plans. Many journals are available on-line; however, you may have to pay a subscription fee to gain access to some of them.

Research skills are very important if planned or guided reading is to be your choice of development activity. It is essential to be able to know what information is available and from where, and know how to draw out the key features of what you read. A disadvantage can be that it is an activity that the learner does alone, and this can make motivation difficult.

Activity 21

Make a brief note of those activities that attracted you, and those you wanted to dismiss as possibilities.

_____

_____

_____

_____

_____

_____

We'll look at the issues raised by your answers to this activity later in this session.

5.8 Access to development activities

The development activities open to you will depend upon the following.

■ Resources available at work – for example a comprehensive training programme may be available, or there could be the facility for using personal computer facilities for working with CD-ROM training packages.
■ Skilled personnel – for example, where experienced individuals are able to coach or mentor individuals.
■ Availability of time and/or financial support – some individuals choose to use their own time at home, or companies sometimes offer individuals financial support to pursue their studies outside work.

Of course, these are not the only reasons why you may, or may not, take up any of the various development activities. But it is important that you know which ones are available and accessible to you, because your development plan (which you will be developing in the next session of this workbook) needs to be valid and reliable. It should not be a wish list of development opportunities, but needs to reflect reality.

5.9 Keeping your objectives in mind

Whatever activities you choose, you need to keep your performance objectives in mind. Constant reference to, and periodic revision of, your development plan will help you to focus on development activities that remain relevant to your particular needs.

6 Ways of learning

Having looked at what's on offer in the world outside, we'll now look at how you yourself like to learn.

The next activity is designed to help you begin to explore your own preferred learning style.

Activity 22

5 mins

Briefly describe any development activity that you have been involved in recently. (For example, was it a training course, or did someone coach you in a particular feature of your job?)

_____

_____

_____

What did the development activity enable you to do and/or know, that you did not do and/or know beforehand?

_____

_____

Summarize briefly what you learned as a result of the activity.

_____

_____

What features of the development activity helped you to learn? (For example, the way the course leader structured the event, using exercises and discussion, or the detailed handouts provided.)

_____

_____

_____

Was there anything you particularly enjoyed, or disliked, about the experience?

_____

_____

Your response to this activity will begin to give you some idea of how you like (or don't like) to learn. What you found helpful and enjoyed about the experience will give you an indication of your preferred way of learning.

For example, the information may have been delivered in a way that you found easy to take in. Or you might have got most out of the information that you were given by using it actively in an exercise. Perhaps you found that, being given the time to reflect on what you had been told enabled you to absorb it more fully. You may have felt stimulated to learn by being with other people, or perhaps you found them a distraction. You may have mentioned more than one reason in your answer.

The development activity you considered in this activity will probably have included one or more of the three main ways of learning:

- imitation;
- instruction;
- experience.

We all use one or other of these ways of learning at different points in life and for different reasons.

As children, we often **imitate** other children or adults we admire and want to resemble; in adult life we might imitate someone whom we feel is a good role model for some form of behaviour ('Now how would So-and-so behave in this situation?'). Or we might imitate how an expert carries out an action ('I see, he holds the mattock with both hands, with one half way down the shaft, and doesn't raise it above his shoulder. Now let me see if I can do that. How does it feel when I do it right?')

We're all familiar with **instruction** as a form of learning from our experience of being taught various subjects at school. In fact, for many people, instruction is learning, and if they've had unsatisfying experiences at school, they're likely to avoid it later if at all possible. However, in adult life, instruction remains an important part of some development activities, such as training courses.

'Experience is the name that everyone gives to their mistakes … Life would be very dull without them.' (Oscar Wilde)

Experience is in some ways a more complex form of learning than the other two, although we learn from experience all through our lives – or don't! This quip highlights the truth that experience alone doesn't necessarily teach us anything. Learning from experience only occurs when you actively think and have feelings about the experience and learn the lessons it provides. A good way of thinking about this process is given in the figure below.

The experiential learning cycle

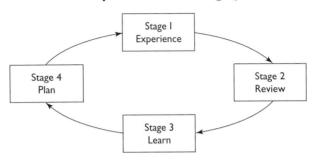

As the name suggests, in stage 1 of the cycle we start with an experience of some kind. Let's take the simple example of waiting for a bus, where we wait for a long time. The second stage involves the learner in reviewing the experience, unravelling the positive and negative features of the experience at stage 1. For example, there was no bus shelter, and it was raining, however, we had an interesting conversation with someone else at the bus stop. At stage 2 we would need to consider what happened, why it happened and the consequences of the experience overall. In this case, we were late for an appointment, we got very wet and spent a few days in bed with a cold, but the long wait also meant that we made a new friend. At stage 3 we identify what we can learn from what happened, by possibly stating:

- 'I should have taken an umbrella …';
- 'I didn't anticipate the problem of being late …';
- 'Perhaps I could have taken the tube …';
- 'I enjoy unexpected meetings with new people …'.

At the fourth stage we plan what we will do next time (e.g. take an umbrella, allow extra time, be more open to the possibilities at bus stops), building on what we have learned from our journey through the experiential learning cycle.

Experiential learning is probably the most effective form of learning, because it involves using all our capabilities in an active way, rather than just accepting what others tell us in a passive way.

6.1 Learning styles

Most of us do not travel equally comfortably through the different phases of the experiential learning cycle. For a number of reasons, we often stay lodged at one or another stage. Some of us are happy to involve ourselves in different experiences, without ever moving forward to review what happened, or to learn from that experience. We enjoy the activity for the sake of the activity, but find it less easy to learn from the experience. Many of us enjoy the process of making plans, but often don't get to the point of putting them into practice.

Each stage of the experiential learning cycle we looked at above is connected with a particular style of learning. The various ways in which people learn were divided by Honey and Mumford into four basic styles.

EXTENSIONS 1 AND 2 You may like to follow up the subject of learning styles by looking at the books by Honey and Mumford listed at the end of this workbook.

- Activist (Stage 1).
- Reflector (Stage 2).
- Theorist (Stage 3).
- Pragmatist (Stage 4).

Spend a few minutes studying the chart below, and think about which most closely resembles your own preferred learning style. (You may have more than one.)

Learning style and brief description
Activist ■ Gets fully involved in new experiences. ■ Enthusiastic about new experiences. ■ Tends to act first, considers the consequences later. ■ Thrives on challenge.
Reflector ■ Likes to stand back and think about what they have experienced. ■ Tends to put off reaching final conclusion as long as possible. ■ Gathers lots of information from lots of different sources – uses this to come to a conclusion. ■ Tends to be thoughtful, considers all angles and implications. ■ Prefers to take a back seat in group situations. ■ Likes to observe others, rather than being involved.
Theorist ■ Takes a logical step-by-step approach to problem solving. ■ Builds facts and establishes theories. ■ Tends to like perfection. ■ Analyses, using principles, models, theories and systems.
Pragmatist ■ Keen to try out new ideas, theories and approaches to see if they work in practice. ■ Experiments with new ideas. ■ Wants to try out new ideas from courses. ■ Acts quickly, confidently where ideas are interesting. ■ Impatient with extended analysis and open-ended discussion. ■ Takes practical approach to problem solving.

Gordon became Customer Service Manager last year. He has attended many different training courses, covering everything from finance to handling conflict. Recently his manager came to him to ask him for a brief evaluation of the courses he had attended.

Gordon realized that he had found the least useful courses to be those that had involved a lot of role-playing and group exercises – he generally left the event feeling that he had wasted his time. He had also attended lectures at the local college and found that where one person was giving out information, supported by handouts and his own notes, he gained a lot of information that he could think about later.

In the course of his evaluation, Gordon noted that: 'I like thinking about the theories and ideas of others, working out where they might work in my department'.

Activity 23

2 mins

Which learning style (or styles) does Gordon prefer?

While it is important to recognize your preferred learning style, it is also important not to box yourself into a corner in doing so. The way we learn most easily naturally influences the forms of development that we choose, and we might ignore ways of learning that are different.

It is also valuable to know your preferred style when it comes to evaluating the effectiveness of any development activity. If you feel that it was not as successful as you had hoped, it could have been because the approach may not have suited your preferred learning style, rather than because there was anything wrong with the activity itself. Gordon is most probably a combination of Reflector and Theorist, but this means that he has tended to dismiss an approach that doesn't fit with these styles of learning.

If you develop a variety of learning styles, you will be able to take advantage of a wider range of development opportunities. Of course, we do not always have the luxury of choice when selecting forms of development to meet our needs. We may have to accept that the opportunity available does not really suit our preferred learning style. However, we can use this self-knowledge to get the most out of what's actually on offer.

7 Barriers to successful learning

As adults we have certain advantages over children when it comes to learning because:

■ we are usually strongly motivated;
■ we have general experience of life.

Our high motivation may come from the desire to succeed, the financial benefits resulting from acquiring new skills, an interest in the subject matter, or simple curiosity.

Experience of things learned in the past makes it much easier for us to learn similar things in the future because we can relate the new to the old, and therefore make sense of it much more quickly.

However, there are certain disadvantages in being an older learner.

Activity 24 · 5 mins

What factors do you think might make it more difficult to learn when we are older? Try to think of four suggestions.

_____

_____

_____

_____

You might have thought of the following:

■ rusty study skills – older learners may be out of practice in carrying out an unfamiliar task, writing notes or memorizing sequences;
■ time limitations – their study time may have to compete with family and social responsibilities;
■ lack of confidence – people who are not used to playing the role of pupil in the pupil/teacher relationship can resent the feeling of subordination, particularly if the teacher is younger than they are;

- poor study environment – there may be a lack of space at home to study in peace, while at work there are often more pressing demands on the learner's time;
- pressure to succeed – failure is much more humiliating when you are older, so the pressure to succeed can be intense;
- previous experience – previous learning can sometimes interfere with new learning.

Activity 25

20 mins

At this point, you might like to begin to check your personal preferences against what is realistic in practice. For example, if you have realized that you need to become more skilled in dealing with conflict in your team, and also that you enjoy a group learning situation, find out if there are workshops available, either locally or through your workplace. If, for whatever reason, this is not realistic, you may need to consider settling for another distance learning workbook on the topic.

The first two sessions of this workbook have helped you to work out what your development needs and performance objectives are, and have examined the range of development opportunities and how these relate to your preferred learning style. With this information, you can now begin to prepare your own personal development plan, and we'll do this in the final session.

Self-assessment 2

10 mins

I Briefly describe the difference between training, learning and development.

_____

_____

_____

_____

_____

_____

2   In order to change a weakness into a strength, you need to set yourself clear
    _____ _____.

3   In order to be effective, you need to be able to set yourself performance
    objectives that are:

    ■ S _____
    ■ M _____
    ■ A _____
    ■ R _____
    ■ T _____.

4   Fill in the missing words in the following diagram.

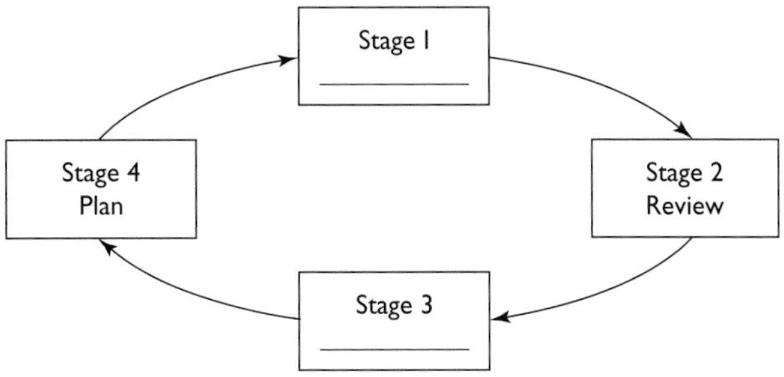

```
                        ┌──────────┐
                        │ Stage I  │
                        │ _____ │
                        └──────────┘
          ┌──────────┐              ┌──────────┐
          │ Stage 4  │              │ Stage 2  │
          │  Plan    │              │ Review   │
          └──────────┘              └──────────┘
                        ┌──────────┐
                        │ Stage 3  │
                        │ _____ │
                        └──────────┘
```

5   List four types of development activity.

    _____

    _____

    _____

    _____

6   You will find a development activity either attractive or unattractive, depend-
    ing on your _____ _____ _____.

7   What are the four basic learning styles?

    _____

    _____

    _____

    _____

    You will find the answers to these questions on pages 134–5.

8 Summary

- The terms 'development', 'training, and 'learning' are used interchangeably, but they do not mean the same things. Training and learning are aspects of development.

- Development is about personal growth and advancement. Training is concerned with learning particular, limited skills. Learning is concerned with understanding and being able to apply the new knowledge in your working life.

- When tackling your training and development needs, you need to divide them into immediate, medium-term and longer-term needs.

- For objectives to be effective, and to reflect your understanding of what you need to be able to do, they need to be SMART: Specific, Measurable, Achievable, Relevant and Time bound.

- A performance objectives states what you will be able to do once you have converted a weakness into a strength. It specifies a development need. Once you have completed a relevant development activity, you will be able to fulfil the performance objective.

- Different forms of development activity will be appropriate for different individuals. No one approach will suit everyone. However, it is important not to rule out forms of development that don't fit with your preferred learning style, otherwise you may miss out on opportunities. The activities that are actually available may not suit your learning style.

- The forms of development activity most commonly available are: training courses and programmes, coaching, mentoring, distance learning, work-based projects, computer-based training, planned or guided reading.

- When deciding on which activities are available to you, you will need to take into account:
  - the resources available at work;
  - whether there are people who are skilled enough to provide coaching or mentoring;
  - the availability of time and/or financial support.

- The four learning styles are: activist, reflector, theorist and pragmatist.

- Older learners experience barriers to learning which they need to recognize and overcome.

Session C
Making it happen

1 Introduction

In the last session you began to look at the different forms of development that might be possible for you, and to examine your own personal learning style. In this session we will construct a personal development plan.

To become more effective, you need to take responsibility not only for producing a development plan for yourself, but also for taking steps to make sure the plan is put into effect.

Once you have turned your plans into reality, you will need to assess their effect. You'll need to ask questions about the value of what you've done, what you now do differently and better, and what you would do differently next time. In order to ask these questions you will need to log, review and examine your development activities in a critical way.

Working through this session will enable you to construct your own personal development plan (PDP), and look at how to put it into practice. It also discusses why it is necessary to review and evaluate your PDP from time to time, and how you can do this.

2 The Personal Development Plan (PDP)

A personal development plan is the result of a process of agreement and discussion. Your manager will probably need to approve the content of your personal development plan, particularly if he or she is responsible for allocating resources for personal and professional development. Your plan may need to be in line with the needs of the department and the organization as well as meeting your own objectives.

We have supplied a format for a PDP that you can either adopt as it stands or adapt for your own purposes. The plan used as an illustration here has been developed around the example of Maddi's development need (see page 29 of Session B), but it is not the only way her performance objective could be met. As you can see, a mix of development forms has been used, with an emphasis on existing resources.

Take a few minutes to look at Maddi's development plan. Obviously it only contains one defined need and objective. For your own PDP, you may need to provide more space to allow for further needs and objectives, or that you want to have different headings.

PERSONAL DEVELOPMENT PLAN

Example

Name: Maddi Edgerns

Job Role: Market Research Phone Team Manager

Line Manager: Arnold Martins

Start Date: 24 April 2002

Development need and performance objective	Achievement of performance objective by	Form(s) of development and resources required/date if available	Method of evaluation for each form of development	Review dates	Comments etc.
Need to give information more clearly so staff can do their jobs.		Team briefing 1 day course (£50 and cover for team supervision) 24 May 02	Brief managers on key learning points from course – 30.5.02	3.6.02	
Conduct weekly briefings, giving out information to all members of the team in a way that enables them to do their job, on a week-by-week basis.	1.7.02	Identify and read up on briefing skills and approaches; copy of 'Presentation Skills for Managers' and handbook produced by marketing team	Production of list of key points to add to those from course – 3.6.02	2.6.02	
		Observe Arnold and two other managers briefing their teams – before 24.5.02 (time away from printshop; excused from writing monthly report)	Discussion on key points raised from observation – 30.5.02	24.6.02	
		Be observed and get feedback from Arnold for two team briefings – 6.6.02 & 20.6.02 (time to review after the event)	Hold discussions with 3 team members who attended the briefing, check they know what they are now supposed to do – review if work carried out as set out at briefing		

Activity 26 · 2 mins

Why is it important to include the kind of detail evident in Maddi's development plan?

What problems could arise if not enough detail is included?

_____

_____

_____

A fully detailed plan will help everyone – yourself and your line manager, and any other relevant people such as your company training manager – to build a clear picture of the **aim** of the development activities. At the same time, it will be immediately obvious what **forms** development will take, as well as indicating what **resources** are needed. The plan can be used as a discussion document when negotiating resources for development.

If a personal development plan does not contain the necessary detail it is all too easy to forget what was intended in the first place. A formal, detailed, agreed personal development plan can provide a practical and valuable source of information and review within the workplace.

Problems that can arise from a personal development plan without enough detail might include:

■ restricted access to the necessary resources;
■ no time for the development activity itself, or for a proper evaluation of it.

Your completed personal development plan should show the **order of priority** of each need and its related **performance objective**. The dates for high priority needs are likely to be fast approaching, and there may also be dates for those that are less urgent. Including definite dates is a good idea, because they will help to focus your mind when you come to review the plan. When drawing up deadlines, it's best to avoid terms like 'ongoing', which are vague, and likely to mean that nothing is ever done about that particular issue.

A personal development plan needs to be seen and treated as a practical working document that is used in discussions (for example, at appraisal and performance review) and which also acts as an organizing reference point – it is an essential document in a manager's working life.

PERSONAL DEVELOPMENT PLAN

Name:

Job Role:

Line Manager:

Start Date:

Development need and performance objective	Achievement of performance objective by	Form(s) of development and resources required/date if available	Method of evaluation for each form of development	Review dates	Comments etc.

Activity 27

S/NVQ
A2

This Activity may provide the basis of appropriate evidence for your S/NVQ portfolio. If you are intending to take this course of action it might be better to write your answers on separate sheets of paper.

Using the PDP form given here (revised if necessary), begin to create a rough draft outline of your own PDP. Depending on your preference, you might want to use either pencil on hard copy (if so, it's useful to make several blank copies), or key it in on screen. Use the list of development needs and performance objectives you have identified in the course of this workbook.

You won't be able to complete the whole form just yet, only the first two columns. As you can see, there are parts of it, in particular methods of evaluation, which we haven't covered yet. As you work through the rest of this session, you will continue to build up your PDP as you go along.

3 From planning to action

Moving from a development plan to a practical development activity is not always quite as straightforward as it might seem. Certainly a plan is the ideal starting point – you have details of what you need to achieve, in the form of one or more objectives. You will also have a list of development activities that you will undertake and resources you will need in order to fulfil the objective(s). Dates for review will also be in place. So what happens next? Well, that's partly up to you!

Your own attitude to the development activity itself is an important factor and will affect its success to some extent. Our personal development is our own responsibility, and it is essential that we take a positive attitude towards it – positive involvement is more likely to result in a positive outcome.

Activity 28

5 mins

Reluctantly, Glyn has agreed with the training department that he needs to develop his presentation skills. He is asked more frequently than before to give presentations both to staff and to clients, and it is an area where he tends to 'fly by the seat of his pants'. The training department has arranged for him to attend a one-day presentation skills course at a local college. The other trainees on the course are from other companies.

Glyn is very busy at work and resents the amount of time that he has to spend away from the office. In addition, one of the other team members made a sarcastic remark about him 'having a day off', which annoyed him. He arrives at the training event in an irritable mood, very aware of the work that will pile up in his absence, and still annoyed at his colleague's sarcasm.

His irritation and resentment mean that Glyn does not get involved in the day, in fact he does his best to stay at the back of the room. His fellow delegates find him negative and obstructive, because he keeps referring to the fact that his absence from work will cause problems for everyone else. The trainer tries to engage his interest, but he is truculent, and makes scathing remarks about the training.

When he completes the evaluation form he states that he has found the day a complete waste of time.

What are the likely effects of Glyn's attitude? What could he have done to make the training event a more positive experience for himself?

_____

_____

_____

_____

We will always find it difficult to learn where we have created obstacles for ourselves – and sometimes we ourselves are the key obstacles that need to be overcome. Glyn needed to agree with his manager and team (and not just with the training department) that the time spent away from the office was essential, even though it may have caused other people immediate problems. Instead of ensuring that everyone knew what he was doing and why, Glyn took his annoyance to the training event and took it out on the people there.

This meant that neither he nor they were able to get as much as they could have done from the day. Not a very constructive attitude! His assessment of the training will be worse than useless, because he hasn't taken a self-critical approach to it but just blamed others.

Time and **support** are two of the resources that could have been specified on his development plan.

Development activity needs to be approached as a positive and challenging experience, if we are to become more effective.

Other people cannot make you develop or improve, this is highly personal, and ultimately you need to be aware of the development opportunities that present themselves and make the most of them.

4 Selecting the right form of development

In Session B we looked at the most common forms of development activity, and by now you probably have a reasonable idea of which ones attract you and which don't. You may also have a pretty good idea about which ones are realistic for you. However, to summarize the important points again briefly: when making the decision about which form of activity is right for you, it may be helpful to run through the following factors with your manager or mentor.

■ The best way(s) of achieving your performance objective.
■ The development opportunities currently available.
■ Your preferred learning style(s).
■ A cost-benefit analysis of resources, i.e. looking at the cost of the resources needed in relation to the benefits of achieving the performance objective.
■ Alternative development opportunities, i.e. those outside the development practices you usually consider.

When you have looked at each of these issues, you will be able to fill in the third column on the PDP form (resources).

The final bullet point above may need some explanation. It is important to remember that development can take place in a range of situations, planned or otherwise, and we need to be aware of these as they arise and incorporate them into our plan if possible. It is part of our responsibility for our own development that we take these opportunities, planned or not, where they will contribute to the achievement of our objectives.

5 Reviewing and evaluating development

Reviewing and evaluating your development plan and your performance objectives is an integral part of all development activity. Without this step, we cannot really know how well we're doing.

Many of us do a training course, for example, intending to improve our communication skills, or practise making presentations. But we often return to work full of good intentions, having given the course a positive evaluation, but have then failed to do very much with what we have learned.

Your development plan should prevent this happening, because you should be able to sit down and review the development activity, either on your own or with someone else. Therefore, reviews need to be noted as important dates and times, either in your diary, on a wall chart, or anywhere that is difficult to ignore.

Activity 29 will help you to ask specific questions of a development activity and its relevance to supporting you in achieving your performance objective(s).

Activity 29 · 2 mins

Ask yourself the following questions in relation to the last development activity that you were involved in.

1a Was the development activity relevant to my performance objective(s)?

Yes/No

1b In what ways was the development activity relevant or irrelevant to my performance objective(s)?

_____

_____

_____

2a   Was there sufficient opportunity and support, back at work,
to put new ideas into practice?   Yes/No

2b   What needed to happen back at work to help me put new ideas into practice?

_____

_____

_____

3a   Was the activity itself suited to my learning style?   Yes/No

3b   What needed to change during the activity to help me work better within my
preferred learning style?

_____

_____

_____

Lack of opportunity to put what's been learned into practice and lack of support back at work following the development activity are often the very things that limit the success of a person's development plan. When listing the resources you will need in your plan, it is essential to include opportunities and support as resources.

Once a full review has been carried out then you may find it necessary to reconsider other development activities that have been included in the development plan. You and your line manager might realize that some planned development activities are not likely to support you in fulfilling your objective. You may decide that other forms of development activity may be more suitable, and your plan will need to be changed to reflect these decisions.

5.1 Evaluating your personal development plan

We can evaluate our plan by how much closer we feel we are to achieving our performance objective. This may be done in a number of ways.

■   Through **personal consideration**, making our own assessment of how close we are to achieving the objective.

■   By **asking others**, e.g. colleagues, team members. Feedback, as explored earlier, is an essential factor in our development. Ask others to describe where they can see improvements in your performance, also ask for suggestions and ideas for further improvement.

- By using **existing measurement techniques in the workplace**. If your organization has procedures for establishing and monitoring quality, use these to find out where your performance has a direct impact on outcomes. For example, suppose the number of customer complaints is published on a weekly basis, and a development activity is offered to staff in order to reduce the number of complaints. We might reasonably assume that a reduction in the published number of complaints is the result of the effectiveness of the development.

You may be able to think of other methods of evaluation.

Activity 30

Decide which forms of review are relevant in your own case and when these might happen. You will probably need to discuss this with a colleague, your manager or mentor.

You can now fill in the fourth and fifth columns of your own PDP form (method(s) of evaluation and date(s) of review).

6 Keeping track

It is important to keep track of your development activities, and one way to do this is by keeping a log of what you do. Keeping a development (or learning) log enables you to:

- compile information for review purposes;
- measure the resources that have been used;
- record types of development activity for future reference.

Professional bodies have various types of membership requirements, and these can involve logging and recording development activity, as part of a continuing professional development strategy. If you belong to a professional organization (or are thinking of becoming a member of one), a development log can provide information to help with your application or with upgrading your membership (e.g. from associate to full membership).

A development log should:

- outline what was involved;
- describe the resources used;
- specify the outcomes (e.g. What can I do differently/better as a result of the activity?);
- consider the effectiveness of the development activity;
- note the time spent on the activity itself.

A development or learning log will be a reliable record of any development activity that you undertake. It can be used to support your application for other jobs, or promotion within your organization, because it shows a logical and comprehensive approach to your own professional development.

The following template is a possible approach to development logging that you might consider using. If you decide to amend the format, make sure that you cover all the detail required, in order to produce a useful and reliable source of information.

DEVELOPMENT ACTIVITY LOG

Type of activity _____

Performance objective that this supports

_____

_____

Briefly outline what was involved, e.g. course attended, article read, etc.

_____

_____

How much did it cost? _____

Were sources of support available? (specify what these were)

_____

_____

Other resources that were needed

_____

_____

How long were you involved in this activity (in hours)? _____

Which skills have you developed as a result of this activity?

_____

_____

What can you now do differently/better that will enable you to achieve your performance objective?

_____

_____

What knowledge have you developed as a result of this activity? How can you apply this knowledge to support the achievement of your performance objective?

_____

_____

What were the positive features of this activity?

_____

_____

What were the negative features of this activity?

_____

_____

Will you use this type of development activity in the future? If yes, why? If no, why not?

_____

_____

Activity 31

Think back to the last development activity that you were involved in and complete a development activity log. Make sure that you have included sufficient detail to provide useful and reliable information for future reference.

7 Revising your PDP

The logging and review process will mean that you can eventually make changes to your personal development plan.

Most obviously, your performance objectives will necessarily change, at least they should once you have succeeded in meeting them! (Or, possibly, you may realize that you wrongly identified what you need to be able to do, and need to redefine them.) If it is to remain a useful and current working document, your performance objectives will need to be revised from time to time. You may also need to revise the dates by which the objectives are achieved, if there are any unexpected problems along the way. It is important to remain very clear about the deadlines, otherwise, if there is a hitch, the deadline will just fade away and nothing will have been achieved.

You may find that a development activity needs to be rethought, or dropped, because:

■ similar activity has not been successful or effective;
■ the performance objective has already been achieved.

Resources may need to be reallocated, in order that you can spend more on one form of development than another, simply because you have found that it is the most effective approach.

The method of review may have to change, or the date, because those involved may not be available for some reason, or you may find the type of review you chose was less helpful than expected.

The Work-based assignment at the end of this workbook will give you the chance to revise your own personal development plan.

7.1 Where do you go from here?

Through your work so far you should be clearer about what you need to do to become more effective in your job. You may have identified a number of areas where you would like to become more effective, and feel rather daunted by the size of the task. The important thing is that you have already made a start.

In deciding where to go from here, you will probably find it most helpful to start on those areas where you will see the most rapid results, and those are likely to be the top priority development needs you identified in Session B. Achieving visible results as soon as realistically possible is the best way to ensure that you continue to take the time and trouble that professional development inevitably entails.

You may have included career moves in your plans, and if so, what you have learned in this workbook will stand you in good stead as you change direction or move further along your present career path. Whatever the case, we wish you the very best of luck in your efforts.

Self-assessment 3

10 mins

1   List the six main items you need to include on a personal development plan.

_____

_____

_____

_____

_____

_____

2   In order for any planned development to be effective, you need to _____ _____ for your own attitude towards it.

3   What factors do you need to take into account when selecting a develop-
    ment activity?

    _____

    _____

    _____

    _____

    _____

4   How can we evaluate effectiveness of any development that we undertake?

    _____

    _____

    _____

5   What does a development, or learning, log enable you to do?

    _____

    _____

    _____

    _____

    _____

6   How does it differ from a personal development plan?

    _____

    _____

    You will find the answers to these questions on pages 135–6.

8 Summary

- Your attitude to development is an important factor and will affect its success.

- Your personal development is your responsibility, other people cannot make you develop or improve.

- Development opportunities may arise in all sorts of ways, so we need to be aware of these as they come up. It is part of our responsibility for our own development that we take these opportunities where appropriate, and where they will contribute to the achievement of our objectives.

- The factors affecting the decision about suitable development opportunities are: the best way(s) of achieving the defined objective; currently available development opportunities; alternative development opportunities; preferred learning styles; resources.

- Reviewing our development activity is not just a useful thing to do, it is essential if we are ever to develop at all.

- We need to evaluate the effectiveness of the development activity, and also how it helps us to attain our performance objective and fulfil our development need.

- Development takes many different forms and so it is important to keep track of the development activities we have undertaken.

- A development, or learning, log should enable you to:

  - outline what was involved;
  - define resources used;
  - specify the outcomes;
  - consider the effectiveness of the development activity overall;
  - note the time spent on the activity itself.

- Any relevant outcomes from the logging and review process should be incorporated into our personal development plan.

Session D
Identifying training needs

1 Introduction

EXTENSIONS 3 AND 4
Two useful texts which explore training needs analysis in greater depth than we can here.

Before any plans or preparations for training can take place, we have to find out what training is needed. It is important that this is done in an organized and systematic manner. If any errors or wrong diagnoses take place at this stage then the results of the training undertaken will not be those needed or desired by the organization.

There are a number of techniques that can be used to identify accurately what training is required. We will look at some of these techniques in this session. We will also examine the skills that the manager will need to use when employing these techniques. For many organizations, identifying training needs is a regular occurrence. Often it can be an annual exercise that follows the business planning process and allows training budgets to be allocated.

The time spent in identifying training needs is time well invested. It will result in training being directed to the areas where it is really needed. It will ensure that the investment made in training is not wasted and that the results are real improvements that make a difference to the operation of the organization.

2 The benefits of training

Any case for training will have to be supported by convincing arguments about the benefits that will result. These have to include business benefits to the organization as well as personal development benefits to the individual.

2.1 Benefits to the organization

Activity 32 · 5 mins

From your own experience and from what we've discussed so far in this session, what benefits can you think of that training brings to the organization? Try to note **two** benefits.

_____

_____

_____

_____

_____

From the organization's viewpoint, training:

- reduces learning time, so bringing new recruits to full working capacity more quickly;
- provides a means of getting jobs done more efficiently, effectively and safely;
- results in a workforce which is more flexible and better able to cope with change;
- improves the morale and motivation of employees, so making them more willing to further the objectives of the organization;
- reduces the number of customer complaints and improves relationships with customers;
- reduces the number of problems with suppliers as goods will be better specified and defects spotted more quickly;
- improves the organization's financial position through increased output or reduced costs.

This last point is the bottom line for any organization. Any investment it makes in training needs to result in an economic gain.

While discussing the benefits of training to an organization it isn't easy to separate those benefits between employers and employees. This is because the benefits aren't all one way – individuals benefit too.

2.2 Benefits to the individual

Sometimes individuals see training as just more work, so you need to be prepared to convince them of the personal benefits. What are they likely to be?

Activity 33 · 5 mins

We've already mentioned some of the benefits of training to individual employees. For the record jot down **three** of these.

_____

_____

_____

_____

_____

You might have mentioned:

■ Increased job satisfaction

Being trained to do a job well generally makes that job much more interesting and satisfying.

■ Improved self-esteem

Trained individuals take more pride in their professionalism.

■   A greater potential for promotion

Increased skills and knowledge make employees more valuable to the organization. Training often gives employees the opportunity to show the organization what they are capable of doing and what their potential is. This encourages organizations to look internally when filling vacancies.

■   Increased opportunities

One skill can act as a basis for learning another. (For instance, someone who has trained to carry out stock taking will be better positioned to become a stock controller in the future.)

This brings us back to the theme of personal development. People at work generally need to feel that they are making progress in some way. Not everyone wants promotion and the responsibility which comes with it. But for most people, it is demoralizing having to do the same job in the same way for a long time.

2.3 Benefits to the manager

Managers obviously benefit from having a well-trained work team. Many of the benefits we have already listed will also be beneficial to the manager, such as:

■   getting work done more safely, efficiently and effectively;
■   improved work team morale;
■   greater flexibility, enabling change to be managed more easily.

But there are more specific advantages for someone like you. For example, how much of your time do you spend 'fire fighting' – dealing with urgent problems which your work team members can't cope with? With better training they might be able to handle things better on their own, rather than having to call on you every time something unexpected happens.

You will probably be happier about delegating responsibility too, if you know that the people standing in for you have been well trained.

And of course, a trained work team is a much more flexible one: people are able to cover for absent colleagues more easily and deal more effectively with unexpected situations.

2.4 Alternatives to training

Consideration of whether to go ahead with training should include an appraisal of the alternatives and the cost and benefits associated with them. Apart from the costs of the training itself – the trainer, the equipment, the accommodation and so on – there is the fact that, while being trained, employees are not working. This sort of lost time is a real concern to any manager. Fortunately on-the-job training and mentoring can greatly reduce the amount of time that a person needs to spend away from work.

Activity 34 · 2 mins

Are there any alternatives to training? Can you think of **at least one** alternative?

_____

_____

_____

_____

Assuming that trained workers are needed, one option for an employer is to only recruit new employees who have already reached the required standards. This is really taking advantage of the training given by others and you will probably have to offer higher wages.

Another alternative is work simplification. At one extreme this can consist of breaking a large job into two or three smaller sections so that it can be tackled by a work team, rather than by an individual. At the other extreme it can mean completely de-skilling a job so that virtually no training is needed to do the work. The disadvantages, however, are considerable and include low employee morale and a high incidence of industrial disputes.

One other alternative is to use subcontracted labour who already have the required expertise. This may be very helpful in the short term but you will have to pay these people at a higher rate.

So in spite of the apparent costs of training, the alternatives are seldom cheaper in the long run. And as we've already seen, the benefits of training are many and varied.

3 The training cycle

We've already discussed the fact that training needs to be carried out in a systematic way to be successful. Now let's be more specific about this.

If the way that things are at present is not the same as the way we'd like them to be, then there is obviously a **performance gap**. Here is a diagram to show these points.

Now the way to improve the skills and knowledge of the work team is through training. Therefore the performance gap is also the extent of the **training need.**

So now we're in a position to spell out the first stage in the training cycle.

3.1 Training cycle stage 1 – Identify the training needs

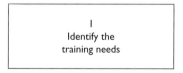

In this first stage you must:

- define the objectives of the work team within the overall objectives of the organization;
- identify the performance gap or training need between what **is** being achieved and what **should be** achieved;
- pinpoint the differences between the **actual** skill levels and the skill levels **needed** for the job.

The whole subject of identifying training needs is discussed in depth later in this session.

The next step is to consider what sort of training programme will meet the training needs.

3.2 Training cycle stage 2 – Making plans and preparations

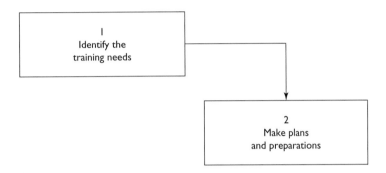

In order to make plans and prepare for training you must be able to:

- define the training objectives;
- identify the course content;
- decide in what order and to what depth it should be learned;
- decide what methods of training are to be used;
- identify who is to learn what;
- plan where and when the training is to take place;
- identify what resources might be needed;
- estimate costs;
- decide who is to support the trainees at work when they come to try out their new skills;
- plan how you will manage to keep the office running while the training is taking place;
- decide who will be involved in giving the training;
- decide how the results will be assessed.

We will consider the answers to these questions in Session E.

Once the plan is in place and the preparations are complete, the training programme can begin.

3.3 Training cycle stage 3 – Implement the plans

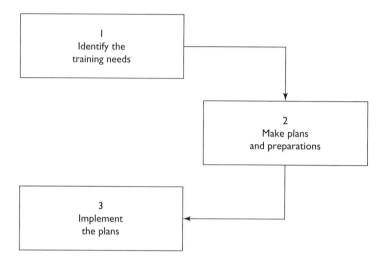

This stage requires you to:

- put the plans into practice;
- ensure the training is carried out, keeping in mind individual needs and individual capabilities;
- be flexible in the approach to training and methods of learning;
- be patient and avoid judging learners too harshly;
- monitor progress carefully and be prepared to make changes to the plans. No plan will survive reality unaltered.

Activity 35

Bearing in mind that this is a cycle we are completing and that the last stage must link back to stage 1, what do you think the final stage of this cycle is?

_____

_____

_____

The last stage is to **evaluate the programme and feed back the results**. As with all well-run projects and programmes, the 'look back and learn' principle should be applied. Otherwise, how will we be able to do better next time?

3.4 Training cycle stage 4 – Evaluate and feed back the results

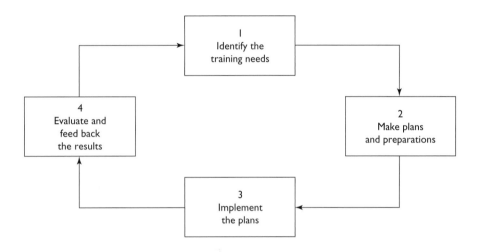

This stage enables you to:

■ measure the performance of the trainees during training and afterwards;
■ check the quality and effectiveness of the training;
■ keep training records;
■ assess job performance;
■ feed back the results to the trainees so they know how well they are progressing;
■ note problems and areas of difficulty.

The evaluation and feedback step is invaluable for everyone involved. It is important to those who:

■ made the plans and prepared the training;
■ gave the training;
■ received the training.

Another reason why feedback is so important is that training can never really come to an end in a working environment. There are always new things to learn. People leave and new people join. Others are promoted, creating both opportunities and learning needs.

4 Types of training need

There are three different types of training need:

- organizational;
- work team;
- individual.

Any training need will be one or another of these.

4.1 Organizational needs

To be fully effective, any analysis of training needs must start with the needs of the whole organization. Some of the key questions of **corporate strategy** that occupy the minds of the top management of any organization are:

- What are the aims of our business?
- What are our strengths and weaknesses?

One of the major strengths or weaknesses of an organization is its workforce. This leads to questions of **personnel planning** such as:

- How well matched is our workforce to the needs of the business?
- What levels of expertise do we have now, and will we need in the future, to achieve our corporate plans?

Organizational needs tend to be defined in broad terms. Many of the objectives need to be broken down and further augmented at a more detailed level before they can be carried out. For many organizational needs this means that they have to be identified at the work team level.

4.2 Work team needs

EXTENSION 5
A useful book for developing and training strategy is *Creating a Training and Development Strategy*, by Andrew Mayo.

Each of the levels below top management will normally be expected to participate in corporate strategy at a departmental or work team level.

Managers of particular departmental functions – such as production, marketing, finance and personnel – will often call upon section heads and work team managers to identify their training needs in relation to the business objectives set for their department or work team. These training needs are expected to be established in the light of the defined objectives of the group in question and the specific problems that it has.

Activity 36 · 10 mins

S/NVQ D7

This Activity may provide the basis of appropriate evidence for your S/NVQ portfolio. If you are intending to take this course of action, it might be better to write your answers on separate sheets of paper.

Think about your own work team. What objectives have been set for them recently? What development will they have to undertake in order to meet these objectives?

_____

_____

_____

4.3 Individual needs

Individual training needs will differ greatly depending on the jobs people are doing and the level of skill they possess. Within a work team of people who are all carrying out the same job, training needs will vary. Some people may already operate and carry out many tasks competently. Other people may have little experience and need to increase their skill and knowledge level. Both these types of people will have training needs but their type and level will differ considerably.

Individual training needs mean just that – they are individual!

There are a number of events which trigger the need for individual training. One is when a new recruit joins the organization. Training needs are also likely to arise when someone:

- moves to a different job, section or department;
- has been selected for promotion;
- has to be instructed in new procedures or safety regulations;
- has been given a new task to carry out;
- is required to cover for another member of the work team.

In fact we can say that individual training needs arise whenever change occurs.

Because change is continual in modern working life and also because 'refresher' training is necessary from time to time, training is needed throughout the working life of most people.

5 Assessing training needs by analysing jobs

We have already introduced the idea of using **performance gaps** to identify training needs. In order to do this you need to compare the way your work team or individual work team members are actually performing with the way you would like them to perform. This requires you to examine or analyse the actual jobs that they are doing.

One way of looking at this is to think of a pair of scales which we need to balance.

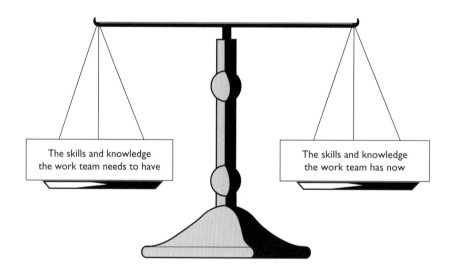

The skills and knowledge the work team needs to have

The skills and knowledge the work team has now

When looking at jobs many organizations now use the national occupational standards forming the basis of the Scottish and National Vocational Qualifications (S/NVQs). These standards lay down the required job performance for most recognized occupations and provide an excellent starting point for any organization to compare their own jobs against.

However, because jobs are not always well defined as S/NVQs, and because they tend to change as time goes by, it may be necessary to carry out a little detective work to find out the real training needs of the work team.

In order to discover the answers to the questions:

- what activities are comprised in the job – what does the job holder actually do?
- what skills are needed to do the job competently?
- does the job holder have all the skills required?

we may need to:

- refer to any available documentation;
- talk to the job holder or the work team;
- observe the job holder in action.

Let's look at each of these options in turn.

5.1 Using documentation

Gwyneth decided to find out whether each work team member was fully trained to carry out their job competently. As she wasn't very familiar with all the work the work team did, she had to think about the best method of discovering what was involved in each job.

Activity 37

3 mins

What kind of documents might be available in an organization that define what's involved in a particular job? Where are such documents likely to be kept?

_____

_____

_____

Some employees complete diaries or work logs, which could be useful as background information. However, the most useful document to be used here would be found in the personnel department. There you would expect to find a **job description** for every job in the organization.

A job description can be defined as:

A broad statement of the purpose, scope, responsibilities and tasks that constitute a particular job.

A job description is a document that describes the activities carried out by the job holder. It also gives other basic data. The list below gives the typical information likely to be included in a job description:

- job title;
- the line manager to whom the job holder reports;
- the main purpose or function of the job;
- the main tasks or duties involved (these should be only the most important duties to be carried out and ideally should not exceed 12);
- details of the work environment;
- any specific responsibilities.

The job description may also include details of:

- department;
- location;
- name of job holder;
- pay details;
- opportunities for promotion;
- unusual conditions;
- the date the job description was written;
- the name of the writer or analyst.

A job description is a snapshot of a job at a particular moment in time. If it is to be used for training needs analysis purposes it is essential that it is current and accurate.

The following is an example of a job description:

Job description			
Job title:	IT Information Developer for Migration Project		
Reports to:	IT Manager		
Responsible for:	Trainee Information Developer		
Based at:	Manningham Road IT Centre		
Main role:	To maintain technical and other documentation produced by Migration developers. Documents will include technical functional specifications and any other technical documents produced by Migration Project.		
Key responsibilities and accountabilities:		**% of job (time)**	**Importance**
1 Identify: ■ new documents being developed by program developers ■ existing documents that need to be updated.		5%	High
2 Receive final version of each new or updated document from authors, then edit for clarity, consistency, completeness and conformity with house style.		75%	Medium
3 Arrange for appropriate people to review and sign off documents.			
4 Send approved copies of documents, together with signed Quality Review forms, to Configuration Manager for filing.			
5 Manage version control.			
6 Archive signed-off version of documents.			
7 Convert signed-off documents into .pdf format and place on Corporate website.		5%	
8 Inform line manager of instances where a new document will have an impact on an existing document.		10%	
9 Send progress reports to appropriate line manager/s at agreed intervals.			
10 Act as scribe at Quality Review meetings.		5%	Low
11 When requested, provide support to authors in using: ■ authoring tools such as MS Word and Visio ■ the Migration template.			

From the job description it should be possible to write down the kinds of qualities, skills and knowledge expected of the job holder.

Activity 38

Briefly note down the qualities, skills and knowledge that you think might be required from someone taking the job of IT information developer as defined in the job description above.

_____

_____

_____

You might have said that people doing this job should be:

■ reliable – because they need to be consistent in checking all documentation which has, or might in the future, change. They are also responsible for reporting regularly on their progress;

■ meticulous – because they are responsible for checking that very complicated technical documents are accurate, consistent and complete;

■ diplomatic – because they need to build good relationships with the authors whose work they are editing;

■ able to work on their own initiative – because they are not working as part of a team, and are not closely managed by their line manager;

■ good communicators – as they also have a training role;

■ familiar with the appropriate software applications (i.e. MS Word and Visio);

■ able to remember complicated facts clearly – because they need to be able to remember the general content of each document.

There are many more skills and qualities which you could have mentioned for a job like this. It would build up to quite a long list.

This statement of the required skills and characteristics (or 'aptitudes') is called a **person profile**, that is it specifies the skills and aptitudes that a person doing that job should have.

By looking carefully at the job description and person profile, you can obtain a good overall understanding of what the job consists of – or at least what it was intended to consist of. You are one step nearer knowing what the training needs are because you now know what you need from the person carrying out this role. Any shortfall from this could be a training need.

However, there are some occasions when it would not be wise to rely entirely on the job description and person profile as your only sources of information about a particular job. Although they are written with the intention of describing the job roles accurately, they may not always do so because:

■ many jobs change over a period of time, and there is often a delay in updating a job description;

■ sometimes the emphasis given in a job description can be rather misleading when it comes to assessing training needs. For example the job description for the information developer emphasized the tasks relating to editing and reviewing the new documents, but one of the most difficult skills to master in such a job is template management – which has only been given a low priority.

5.2 Using discussion

Keep people informed about what you are doing and why.

When discussing training needs with a job holder the first thing to inform them about is **what** you are doing and **why**. You will need their involvement and co-operation to proceed and so it is vital to gain their commitment at this stage.

You may choose to have this discussion with the work team or privately with each individual. However you choose to carry out the discussion you will need to ensure that the information you receive is of the right quality and quantity. To do this you will need to adopt a constructive questioning approach.

To ask constructive questions you will need to ask **open** questions. These are questions that people cannot answer with just a 'yes' or a 'no'. They require them to give some information and join in a discussion. Open questions are very useful for establishing rapport, opening up topics or discovering feelings. Very often this type of question will begin with the words:

■ What?
■ Where?
■ Why?
■ Who?
■ When?
■ How?

You might ask questions like:

What activities take up most of your working day?
What ideas have you got about …?
How do you feel about …?

5.3 Observing the job holder

The next obvious step, if you are still in doubt about what is involved in the job, is to observe the job holder in action.

This can be done formally or informally.

■ Formal observations

This would happen if you put aside a set period of time, perhaps a day or so, and sit or stand near to the job holder and watch what tasks are performed. While watching you would also make notes of what you see.

■ Informal observations

As part of the normal routine you will usually observe your work team in action. You can therefore observe them over a period of time without seeming to do so. You should not take notes when you are observing informally.

Activity 39 · 3 mins

Can you think of **one** advantage and **one** disadvantage for each method of observing the job holder?

Formal observation:

_____

_____

Informal observation:

_____

_____

If you are observing people formally some of the advantages are that it allows you to discuss the process with the job holder and explain the reasons for carrying out the observation. The job holder is then able to prepare him/herself for the event. It also enables you to put aside set time to carry out the observation.

Some of the disadvantages are that people do not always behave normally when they are being watched – they may feel that they should do what they're expected to do, rather than what they usually do. Another problem is that it may arouse feelings of resentment.

You may have mentioned some of the following advantages of observing informally. It allows managers to spread the time needed for the task of observation over a period of time and it also allows them to get more involved with the work of the work team.

Some disadvantages of this method, however, are that is it not such a systematic approach and thus may not be so accurate. Managers may also find themselves distracted from the task by other events and so not accomplish it.

Observation allows managers to analyse a task because it allows them to see it actually being carried out. It also allows managers to assess the competence of the person carrying out the job. This can be extremely useful when analysing training needs.

6 Training needs analysis by task

In order to specify training needs very precisely, it may be worthwhile analysing jobs task by task. The chart shows how this was done with a receptionist.

Task Analysis Assessment Chart		
Job title	**Receptionist**	
Job holder	**Debbie Wilson**	
Task description	*Knowledge/Skill Required*	*Proficiency reached and training advised*
Task 1: **Dealing with visitors**	Skill in dealing with callers, trades people, job applicants etc.	Carried out efficiently. No further training required at this time.
Task 2: **Operating the telephone switchboard**	Skill in handling callers, knowledge of and skills at operating switchboard, knowledge of organizational procedures in handling callers.	Job holder not fully conversant with new switchboard operation – training needed. Not familiar with procedures for handling difficult callers – instruction needed (if procedures exist).
Task 3: **Operating the computer to access status of stock figures for organizational sales staff**	Skills in and knowledge of computer inputting and interpreting display.	Does a reasonable job in spite of lack of training. Background training in system operation would aid understanding.
Task 4: **Typing when not busy**	Skills in typing.	Not very good. Job holder is not a trained typist. External training could be recommended but frequent interruptions mean this aspect of the job may have to be re-evaluated.

Activity 40

15 mins

S/NVQ
D7

This Activity may provide the basis of appropriate evidence for your S/NVQ portfolio. If you are intending to take this course of action, it might be better to write your answers on separate sheets of paper.

You may like to try your hand at analysing a job using our chart. For this activity pick a job that you are very familiar with but that is also one that you know you will be required to arrange some training for in the near future. List three or four tasks that are included in the job and summarize the **skills** and the **knowledge** required for each task. Then make a judgement about how well the task is being performed and suggest any training you feel would help the job holder in performing the task better.

Task Analysis Assessment Chart		
Job title		
Job holder		
Task description	*Knowledge/skill required*	*Proficiency reached and training advised*
Task 1:		
Task 2:		
Task 3:		
Task 4:		

You may not have found this activity too easy to do. In a real-life situation, you may spend quite some time analysing a particular job before you feel you can properly assess the training needs. And, of course, training needs analysis is not something you do once and forget about.

A workteam either develops or stagnates.

It isn't usually a question of 'clearing up all the training needs' and then forgetting all about training. Training never stops. Once you've identified the needs of your work team and instituted one training programme you will probably find yourself having to think about the next lot of training. Don't forget that a work team either develops or stagnates.

Training is one way to help your work team continue to develop.

7 Other training needs identification techniques

The remainder of this session will explore other ways of identifying and agreeing training needs.

7.1 Versatility charts

Coping with unexpected absence is a problem nearly every manager has to deal with from time to time. It may be caused by a temporary absence like sickness, but it may be of a more permanent nature, like an employee suddenly leaving.

A manager who can cope without too many difficulties in this kind of situation probably has a well-organized and well-trained work team. Having the capacity to deal with absence depends upon:

- good communications and a good record-keeping system, so that the work team and the manager are not too reliant on information that is only carried around in the head of the absentee;
- having people trained to do more than one job.

What about training? How can a manager be sure that there is enough cross-training among work team members so that absenteeism won't normally result in an unacceptable level of disruption?

The easy way to find out is to make a versatility chart that shows who's trained in what. In simple terms a versatility chart is an employee/job matrix which lists all the individuals from a work team across the top of a grid and lists all the main departmental tasks down the side. Against each name the manager can mark the tasks that each individual is able to perform using a code such as the following:

M   main person normally undertaking this task
S   person required to stand in
C   person is competent to carry out the task

Gwyneth's work team consisted of eight people, seven of whom worked in the General Office. Felix was her Chief Clerk and he had been with the work team the longest. Gwyneth realized that if Felix went sick there would be no-one to cover for him. She decided she had better make a summary of which work team members were trained to do what jobs. She drew up the following versatility chart.

Versatility Chart							
	General Office Staff						
	Jean	Felix	Martha	Aracea	Cathy	Eddie	Max
Wages		S C		S C	S C	M C	S C
Purchase ledger		S C		M C			
Sales ledger			S C	S C	M C		
Stock control	S C		M C	S C	S C	S C	M C
Work allocation		M C					
Control and checking		M C					
Customer complaints		M C	S C				
Payment authorization		M C					
Customer enquiries		S C	M C			S C	
Data input	S C	S C	S C	M C	M C	S C	M C
General admin	M C	S C	S C	S C	S C	S C	S C
Word processing	M C						

To complete the final estimate with the versatility chart Gwyneth will need to calculate the following.

a How many people carry out this job competently at the present time?
b How many competent people are required with skills in this area to ensure adequate cover?
c How many people are currently competent to stand in for this task?

The number of people requiring training, which we will call (d), is worked out as follows:

$$b - (a + c) = d$$

Activity 41

5 mins

Using the information provided below work out (d), the number of people who require training in each task. Sometimes the calculation will produce a minus figure (see Wages). That means there are more than enough people to cover the task and the number requiring training is zero.

Training Required				
	Calculation			
Task	a	b	c	d
Wages	1	2	4	0 (−3)
Purchase ledger	1	3	1	
Sales ledger	1	3	2	
Stock control	2	4	5	
Work allocation	1	2	0	
Control and checking	1	2	0	
Customer complaints	1	2	1	
Payment authorization	1	2	0	
Customer enquiries	1	4	2	
Data input	3	5	4	
General admin	1	4	6	
Word processing	1	3	0	

Answers to this Activity can be found on page 137.

You will see that it's possible to tell quite a lot from a simple versatility chart. The chart is easy to draw up and very useful when it comes to rearranging cover for different job functions.

Of course it won't tell the manager who to train to cover for the necessary tasks. That will be a matter of considering things such as:

- the present workload of the employees;
- their existing skill levels;
- their ability to learn new tasks;
- their willingness to learn new tasks.

Activity 42

S/NVQ D7

This Activity may provide the basis of appropriate evidence for your S/NVQ portfolio. If you are intending to take this course of action, it might be better to write your answers on separate sheets of paper.

Complete the versatility chart below for your work team or section.

Versatility Chart							
Jobs or tasks	Work team or section member						

Once you have completed the versatility chart you will now be able to decide which tasks or jobs require additional cover.

Training Required				
Task	Calculation			
	a	b	c	d

You will now be able to decide who should undertake the training required to make this additional cover available.

Although versatility charts are often useful, they do not always give a complete picture of training needs.

Activity 43

Can you think of one work situation where a versatility chart would **not** tell a manager everything he or she needs to know about work team training needs?

_____

_____

_____

Versatility charts don't tell you about the training needs beyond the normal job functions of the work team.

- Safety training, for example, may require a completely separate training programme.
- Versatility charts assume that one task consists of skills that can be learned in a reasonably short period of time by another work team member. This is by no means always true. Some skills can only be learned after years of practice.
- They don't allow for the range of skills and knowledge that one job might encompass, nor do they give any indication of the degree of expertise required by the job holder.

7.2 Diff-rating scales

A diff-rating scale works by specifying tasks and rating them according to whether you consider them to be:

- important;
- carried out frequently;
- difficult to learn.

This scale should help you to decide which training should be given priority. Here is an example of a diff-rating scale.

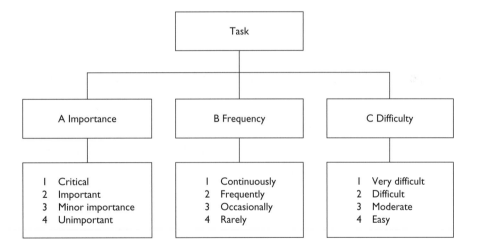

It is possible to take a task and to give it a rating of 1 to 4 for each of the three categories A, B and C.

Activity 44

5 mins

What training recommendations would you make for the following tasks that have been given the following ratings?

Task	Rating	Training recommendation
Task 1	A4, B4, C4	
Task 2	A1, B1, C1	
Task 3	A1, B4, C4	
Task 4	A1, B4, C1	

- **Task 1**

  This task does not require any training as it is unimportant and rarely carried out. It is also easy to learn and should be picked up when needed without any specific training.

- **Task 2**

  This task needs immediate training as it is a critical task and one that is carried out continuously. It is, however, very difficult to learn and this will need to be taken into account when planning the training.

- **Task 3**

  Training should be undertaken in this example as it is a critical activity. However, as it is rarely carried out, a one-off training session may not suffice and regular refresher training may be needed. This should not be too difficult to arrange as the task is an easy one to learn.

- **Task 4**

  Immediate training should be arranged for this task as again it is a critical activity. However, the planning will need to take into account the fact that it is not an easy task to learn and that it is rarely used at work. This means that lots of practice will not be available at work and will need to be included in the training.

7.3 Appraisal interviews

Another method used to identify training needs is the formal performance appraisal interview which provides a useful opportunity to discuss training needs with an individual. It gives work team members the chance to say what training they think they need or would like. It also gives managers an opportunity to explain what training is available or is planned.

Performance appraisal is a method of evaluating a work team member's progress and performance. It is usually conducted as part of an annual formal interview.

In many companies employees are encouraged to prepare for this interview by completing a pre-appraisal questionnaire. This makes them think about such issues as:

- self-assessment of past performance;
- strengths and weaknesses;
- areas for improvement in the future;
- key objectives for the next year;
- ambitions for the future;
- training needs.

The employee is then able to participate more actively in the interview. You can learn more about appraisals in the workbook *Motivating to Perform in the Workplace*.

8 Agreeing and recording identified training needs

It is an important part of your role to identify accurate training needs. However, the task is not completed at this stage. The training needs must be agreed and approved, perhaps by both your line manager and the individuals in question. Having reached agreement it is then essential for the agreement to be recorded. This will allow you to move on to the next stage in the training cycle – that of planning and preparing for the training.

8.1 Agreeing training needs

We mentioned above that it is possible that two different people will need to be consulted to agree training needs.

■ The work team member

In Session A we said that the commitment and motivation of individuals is essential if training is to be effective. This means that the individuals need to recognize the need for the identified training. For this recognition to occur you will need to discuss training needs with the individual. We have already suggested that discussion is one way of identifying training needs anyway, but this discussion may need to be held after you have reached some conclusions.

The discussion will also enable you to talk over with the individuals any personal circumstances or special learning requirements they may have.

Activity 45

S/NVQ D7

This Activity may provide the basis of appropriate evidence for your S/NVQ portfolio. If you are intending to take this course of action, it might be better to write your answers on separate sheets of paper.

Can you think of an example of when a discussion about training needs with one of your work team has resulted in you modifying your recommendations for training? Give details below.

Ask the employee involved to sign a statement to say that this is a true record of what took place.

_____

_____

_____

_____

■ Your line manager

There may be several occasions when you might need to refer to a higher level of management for guidance on analysing training needs. For example you might need to talk about:

■ information on organizational or work team objectives;
■ details of training budgets available;
■ guidance on stand-in cover requirements;
■ policy on techniques to use when identifying training needs;
■ advice on problems encountered.

If you are compiling an S/NVQ portfolio, and have a specific example of when you have needed guidance, write a record of the circumstances and ask the manager involved to sign it. You may then be able to use this as testimony evidence.

8.2 Recording training needs

Once agreement has been reached the next step is to record that agreement. There is no set way of doing this, although it is important that it is in writing.

A short memo, letter or report giving details of the final decisions arrived at is all that is needed before moving on to the planning and preparation stage.

In this session we have given you two examples of ways in which training needs can be recorded:

- a task analysis assessment chart as used in Activity 40
- the training recommendation form used with the versatility chart in Activity 42.

This concludes the task of identifying training needs and allows the record to be passed on to the relevant personnel. We can now start stage 2 of the training cycle in Session C.

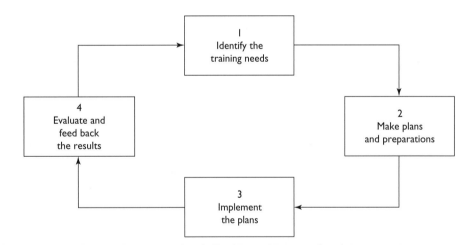

Self-assessment 4

20 mins

Complete the crossword below using the clues given.

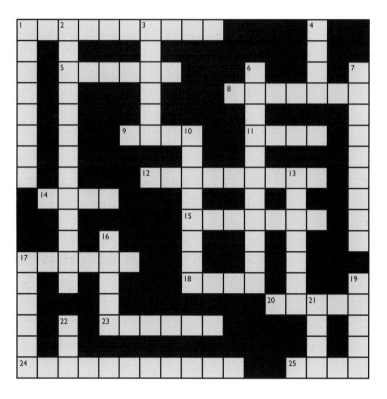

Across

1 One of the three types of training need. (10)
5 Training will always be needed when this is happening. (6)
8 If work teams don't do this they will stagnate. (7)
9 Training needs may affect the whole work ----. (4)
11 Training needs analysis is a systematic method and should be completed ---- by step. (4)
12 The training at the beginning. (9)
14 Versatility charts show the ---- person normally undertaking a task and the person required to stand in. (4)
15 and 4 down It is important that managers ------ what the ---- benefits of training are. (7, 4)
17 The question that it's OK to say no to. (6)
18 See 3 down. (4)
20 When being observed formally some job holders ------ in a resentful way. (5)
23 When analysing jobs and tasks it is important to look at both ------ and knowledge. (6)
24, and 1 and 16 down Part of the ----------- job is to -------- training ------. (11, 8, 5)
25 Because of organizational needs it is not always possible to give individuals the training they -----. (4)

Down

1 See 24 across. (8)
2 The job description is this. (13)
3 and 10, and 18 across Diff-rating scales work by rating the ------ of difficulty in a task. Tasks are rated as very difficult, difficult, -------- or -----. (6, 8, 4)
4 See 15 across. (4)
6 and 17 The matrices that help identify training needs. (11, 6)
7 The annual interview that monitors progress. (9)
10 See 3 down. (8)
13 and 21 You should try to ------- job holders in their own ---- of work. (7, 4)
16 See 24 across. (5)
17 See 6 down. (6)
19 It's important at the ----- of the identification process to decide what methods are to be used. (5)
21 See 13 down. (4)
22 The performance --- identifies the training need. (3)

Answers to this crossword can be found on page 136.

9 Summary

■ Training benefits the organization, the individual and the manager.

■ The training cycle has four stages and can be represented as follows:

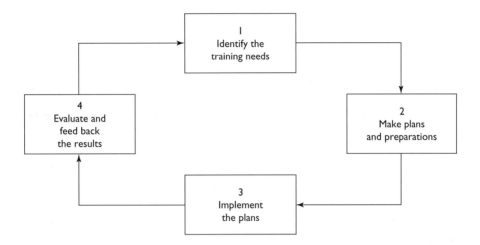

■ Training needs arise from three sources: **organizational** needs, **work team** needs and **individual** needs.

■ Training needs can be **analysed** by:

   ■ referring to any available documentation, including job descriptions;
   ■ talking to job holders;
   ■ watching the job holder in action;
   ■ carrying out a formal performance appraisal interview.

■ Individual training needs arise whenever **change** takes place.

■ Training is one way to help your work team continue to **develop**.

■ **Training needs identification techniques** include:

   ■ job analysis;
   ■ task analysis;
   ■ versatility charts;
   ■ diff-rating scales;
   ■ performance appraisal interviews.

Session E
Planning successful training

1 Introduction

EXTENSION 6
For help in designing clear training objectives and much more, read *How to Write and Prepare Training Materials.*

As with so many management activities **planning** is the key to success.

This is certainly true of training. To be effective it must be carefully thought out in a logical and clear way. At the beginning we need to have clear objectives. We need to have a precise understanding of what we are trying to achieve. Once we are clear about this we can then start looking at the details of the training.

We need to look carefully at the training methods to be used and to consider which methods would assist with the learning. We also need to plan the content of the programme to ensure that it is logical and sequential and that the most important elements are included. All the administrative arrangements must be carried out to ensure facilities, equipment, materials and trainees are available. And finally we need to plan the way in which we aim to evaluate the effectiveness of the final result.

Induction training is a good example of training that needs to be well planned. A new employee's introduction to the organization needs to contain everything that the person will need to know in order to settle down quickly and fit in. It is not something that will just happen, nor will it be complete and interesting if it is not planned.

During this session we will look at each of these issues in turn.

2 What are we trying to achieve?

When drawing up plans start at the end.

When drawing up plans and projects, it's best to start at the end.

What we mean by this apparently paradoxical statement is that any plan or project must have a purpose (or end) and, until you are clear about what you are trying to achieve, you can't expect to succeed.

What's more, before you start, you need to know how to **measure** the success of your venture. Otherwise, it may be difficult to know whether it has succeeded.

To do this thoroughly you need a defined method of measurement. Writing training objectives will provide you with this necessary measure.

When writing objectives it is important that they conform to the SMART principle. This states that objectives should be:

When writing objectives use the SMART principle.

S   pecific
M   easurable
A   chievable
R   elevant
T   ime bound

■ Specific

Training objectives must be precise and exact in explaining what is to be achieved. This means that the specific objectives of a particular training programme must be defined in terms of the desired improvement in work performance. Specific objectives should describe both **performance** and **standards**, i.e. what is to be done and how well it is to be done.

■ Measurable

The purpose of setting objectives is to enable some measurement of success to take place. This means that objectives must be written in terms that are easy and possible to measure.

■ **Achievable**

Objectives should only state what it is reasonable to expect the trainee to achieve. It would not, for example, be realistic to expect someone to pass a driving test after just one lesson. This could not be achieved in the timescale. Again, if the necessary resources were not available, the objective would not be achievable.

■ **Relevant**

The training objectives set must be relevant both to the work the trainees are carrying out and to the training content of the programme. There is no point in teaching someone spreadsheets if they are only going to be involved in word processing.

■ **Time bound**

Training objectives should clearly state the time in which the trainee is expected to achieve the desired results. If the programme is a one-week course are they expected to achieve the results at the end of that time? Will they need further practice? If so, how much longer might this be reasonably expected to take?

Activity 46 · 10 mins

Examine the training objectives of the one-day training course below. Decide whether you think they meet the SMART principles.

1   Understand the basic principles of health and safety.   Yes/No

2   Conduct health and safety audits to meet the standards of the Health and Safety Executive.   Yes/No

3   At the next team meeting explain clearly their management responsibilities under the Health and Safety at Work Act.   Yes/No

4   Draw up an accurate plan of their area of work showing where all fire exits and fire extinguishers are located in readiness for the next safety committee meeting.   Yes/No

Objectives 3 and 4 are both good objectives. They are specific, measurable, achievable, relevant and time bound.

Objective I is not measurable because the verb used ('understand') is not measurable. The objective should be written using a verb such as 'state' or 'explain', so that the learner has to do something which can actually be seen and measured.

Objective 2 is not an achievable objective. In a one-day course it would be impossible to achieve the standard set.

Activity 47 · 15 mins

Imagine that you have been asked to design an induction programme for your organization or section. This is a programme that all newcomers to the organization or section will need to go through. Write down the training objectives you would choose.

_____

_____

_____

_____

_____

You may have included objectives like these.

At the end of the induction training newcomers will be able to:

- accurately complete the organization chart;
- fully explain the organizational mission statement;
- quickly locate the staff canteen, rest rooms and medical centre;
- explain the main features of the organization's policy on paid and unpaid leave.

In addition to writing objectives you will have to give some thought to the people you are designing the training programme for. You will need to consider their:

- current competence;
- potential competence;
- learning ability;
- work activities.

You will also need to consider what skills:

- you require the individual to have;
- you require the work team to have;
- the organization may require of the individual or the work team in the future.

Activity 48

S/NVQ D7

This Activity may provide the basis of appropriate evidence for your S/NVQ portfolio. If you are intending to take this course of action, it might be better to write your answers on separate sheets of paper.

Consider one member of your work team who has a training need over and above induction training. What are his or her current and potential competence, learning ability and work activities? Use the chart below as a framework for your thinking.

Initial Assessment Plan
Name of work team member and details of training need:
Assessment of current competence:
Assessment of potential competence:
Assessment of learning ability:
Details of work activities:
Signed _____ Date _____

3 The way people learn

Why is it that some things you are told just don't stick, yet other things which are useful or important to you are there for life as soon as you have learned them?

3.1 Participative learning methods

Compare these two learning situations.

1 You are attending a lecture on a subject that doesn't really interest you and that doesn't seem to be very relevant to what you do at work.

2 You are taking part in a discussion with an expert on a topic which has a great deal of bearing on your everyday work activities and which you find very interesting.

The main differences between these two learning situations are that:

- the subject of the lecture **is not relevant** to what you do but the subject of the discussion is.
- the subject of the lecture **does not interest you** but the subject of the discussion does.
- the lecture is a passive training situation that **you are not able to get involved in** apart from listening, but you can **take an active part in** the discussion.

In these circumstances you are more likely to learn from the discussion than from the lecture.

This illustrates three important principles of learning:

People learn better when they:

- **can relate what they are studying to something they already know and understand;**
- **are interested in the subject being taught;**
- **take part actively in the learning process, rather than simply listening or watching passively.**

Activity 49

Imagine you are instructing members of your work team about a new job. It is important that the work team members learn and remember certain information.

Tick **one** box to show whether you think it would be better to:

- collect the information yourself and present it to the work team members or ⬚

- get them to find out the information for themselves. ⬚

From the learning point of view, it would be far better to encourage the work team members to seek out the information for themselves because:

People learn better when they discover information for themselves rather than being presented with it.

3.2 Learning styles

As you learnt in Session B, when learning any new piece of knowledge or skill a learner needs to go through four separate stages (rather like the training cycle). These stages make up the learning cycle, which can be illustrated as follows.

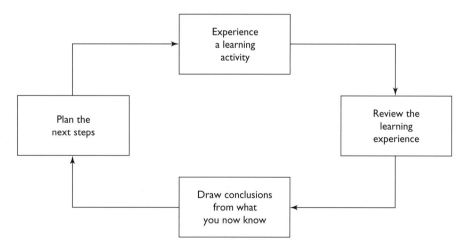

Although there is no best way of learning it is possible for the trainee to join the learning cycle at any stage and learners usually have one (or possibly two) stages within the learning cycle where they prefer to start. These stages are their preferred **styles of learning**. Let's look at four trainees with different preferred styles of learning.

Stephen Bryant likes to learn in an active way – he likes to learn by doing. He is not afraid of making mistakes and will try anything once. He has an 'activist' style of learning.

Jean Walsh likes to stand back and think about things before she tries them out. She likes to collect information and data and carefully analyse it before she applies it in practice. She has a 'reflector' style.

Graham James likes to adapt information gained and put it into sound logical theories. He likes to gather facts together, and is keen on basic principles and models. He needs to be given the basic theories before he can start to think about how they can be applied in practice. He has a 'theorist' style.

Margaret Hill is a very practical person who likes to try out ideas and theories to see how they work in practice. She needs to take ideas and then plan how they can be applied before she actually tries them out. She has a 'pragmatist' style.

Activity 50

5 mins

Consider two members of your own work team. What preferred styles of learning do you think they have and what are the reasons for your choice? Record your answers in the space provided.

Work team member	Learning style preferred	Reasons

Once you have identified the learning styles of individuals, what should you do about it? Well, it might affect the training methods you plan to use. For example a theorist might prefer a more formal training session, whereas an activist might prefer some practical training.

4 Training on or off the job?

Both on-the-job training and off-the-job training have advantages and disadvantages. They can usefully be combined to create a comprehensive training programme.

4.1 Training on the job

One common approach to job training is the 'sit by Nellie' method. You probably know the kind of thing.

'Oh, you must be the new starter. Here, come and sit by Nellie for a few days. She'll show you the ropes.' And Nellie, being a patient and kind person and used to 'showing the ropes' to trainees, tries her best to pass on her skills and knowledge. At least we hope she does.

In truth, if the job really is simple and can be learned quickly by most people then the 'sit by Nellie' system often works well enough. Otherwise it does have its drawbacks.

Activity 51

Can you think of **two** disadvantages to the 'sit by Nellie' approach to training?

_____

_____

_____

There are a number of disadvantages, even if Nellie enjoys being used in this way and makes every effort to be a good trainer.

■ Nellie may not have received any formal training herself, either in the job or in the skills of training.
■ The 'watch me do this' method can omit any explanation to the trainee about the underlying principles involved.
■ The training may be unstructured, not planned and not prepared.
■ An unskilled trainer may pass on bad habits as well as good ones.
■ The 'pool of knowledge' in the work team may diminish after time because of a lack of fresh ideas and a dilution of skills.
■ Mistakes made can be very costly.

Mistakes can be very costly.

You probably came up with still more drawbacks to the system.

If you are currently using the 'sit by Nellie' approach you may want to ask yourself if you can improve the learning techniques but still allow trainees to learn on the job.

Activity 52

5 mins

What circumstances need to be present in an on-the-job training programme to ensure its success? Try to list at least **three** things.

_____

_____

_____

_____

Some of the circumstances you may have mentioned are these.

■ The people undertaking the training should themselves be trained, not only in the job but also in training skills.
■ There should be a structured, planned and prepared training programme, which includes some explanation about the underpinning knowledge and theories.
■ A number of different trainers need to be involved in the training.
■ Adequate time must be built into the programme for practice.

Well-planned and well-prepared on-the-job training takes a lot of time to organize if it is to be done well. But it can also result in excellent outcomes. Training provided on the job is often seen as being more relevant and directly related to the job the person is doing.

4.2 Training off the job

Training away from the job also has a number of benefits, such as giving:

■ a better chance to think clearly and to concentrate away from the noise and the bustle of the workplace;
■ freedom from interruption and from the pressures of work;
■ an opportunity to practise where it does not matter if mistakes are made;
■ an opportunity to think through the principles behind actions and perhaps to question why the work is done in the way it is.

As with on-the-job training there are some disadvantages with this method of training. Off-the-job training requires people to be away from work for periods of time, it requires the provision of training facilities such as a room and flipchart, and it often has to rely on simulation-type practice.

5 Choosing the best method

There are numerous methods of training. Your choice will depend on:

■ the needs of your trainee(s);
■ the demands of your task;
■ the constraints of your budget;
■ the resources you have available.

This section will introduce some of the more commonly used techniques so that you can decide which ones you would like to build in at the planning stage.

Some methods, such as demonstrations, will normally take place at work, but on the whole these methods can be used flexibly in the workplace or away from the immediate pressure of the job.

■ **Demonstrations**

The purpose of a demonstration is to pass on skills by imitation and practice. It differs from the 'sit by Nellie' approach in that it is planned, and is combined with clear explanations of what's involved and the reasons behind the actions.

The procedure is best carried out in the following four stages:

- preparation
- introduction
- demonstration and explanation
- practice.

■ **Coaching**

Coaching is sometimes thought of as an extension of the demonstration technique already described. However, it is also a process of developing the experience and abilities of partially trained individuals through:

- issuing specific, planned tasks that are assessed on completion;
- continuously monitoring and appraising progress;
- holding regular review sessions.

■ **Presentations and discussions**

A presentation is a prepared speech, and is usually followed by discussions on specific topics.

Presentations are a way of imparting information to a group rather than simply to individuals. They can be used for a variety of purposes besides giving direct job instructions, for example, for conveying news about the organization.

The idea of a discussion is to get a group of people actively participating in learning.

■ **Videos and DVDs**

You may have access to training videos or DVDs. These can be very helpful training aids, provided they are well made and relevant.

Their main advantage is that, as the saying goes, 'a picture can be worth a thousand words'. It is possible to show on video or DVD what cannot otherwise be seen, perhaps showing a process in slow motion or an interview or appraisal situation which would normally take place in private.

One disadvantage is that they can quickly become out of date.

The best way to use videos and DVDs is to combine them with another form of training. It's a good idea to hold a discussion session immediately after a video showing, in order to review and reinforce ideas.

■ Mentoring

A mentor is a person who agrees to act as an adviser or guide to a person with less experience than themselves. The general aim is to help the inexperienced person to develop his or her long-term goals.

■ Open/flexible learning

We shouldn't forget the method you are using for training at the moment – open/flexible learning.

Open/flexible learning has several advantages, assuming you can find a course suitable to your needs. These advantages include:

■ working at your own pace, in your own time and wherever suits you best;
■ interactive design, so that you can respond to questions and activities and are given feedback and analysis.
■ the frequent use of printed materials, which are easily portable and accessible anywhere, relatively cheap and may be preferred by some users to working on screen.

■ E-learning

E-learning is a type of open learning in which the information is displayed on a computer screen rather than on paper. The training is normally interactive, i.e. the program contains information, case studies, assessment tests, etc. and learners are able to input responses via their keyboards.

The main formats are as follows.

■ Computer-based training (CBT) packages – These are interactive learning programs which contain text, diagrams and, often, audio and video. They provide information, interactive exercises, assessment and feedback. CBTprograms can be loaded onto a PC from the Internet, from the organization's own intranet, a CD-ROM disk or, increasingly in the future, from a DVD.

The benefits of CBT include the fact that it is usually developed in a modular format, i.e. the subject matter is presented in separate modules that can be studied alone or as part of a series and, from which either the trainer or the learner can select the topics required for a particular course. The learners can learn at a time convenient to them, and take as long as they need. Possible drawbacks are that they will need a PC, and some people find that they become isolated and demotivated if they are not working in a group. Again, unless you can arrange for tutorial support to be provided, there is no one to ask if things go wrong.

■ Online reference manuals – reference documents, such as operations manuals, can be accessed online in .pdf format by anyone who has Adobe Acrobat Reader software on their PC. Again, this format is not interactive.

■ PowerPoint presentations – these are useful for displaying diagrams and other important points for a presentation. They can be delivered to learners via the organization's intranet or projected from the computer onto a wall screen by means of a projector. They are not interactive, i.e. the learner cannot key in information, select options from a menu or answer on-screen assessment questions.

6 Planning the training

Let's assume that you have decided on:

■ the objectives of the training programme;
■ methods of participative learning and learning styles;
■ location of the training;
■ training methods;
■ visual aids.

Planning well means getting the detail right. To complete the planning of your training there are still a few items that need to be considered. In this section we will look at the finishing touches that will ensure your training programme can be delivered effectively. These are:

■ course content and order of presentation;
■ timing;
■ facilities and equipment.

6.1 Course content

The content of the course will depend on your organization and the needs of your work team. If we take the induction course as an example, you would normally include such topics as: company rules, health and safety rules, location of fire exits, fire drills, a company tour, introductions to other staff, pay details, pension rights, holiday entitlement, car parking, training available and details of the job.

You may find that you need to:

- revise your own knowledge and understanding of the subject (you will probably find that you learn a lot more when you come to do the training; trying to teach something is an excellent way of learning it);
- break down the material into manageable chunks;
- go through things stage by stage, bearing in mind what the trainees do and do not know;
- work out how you are going to explain difficult points;
- plan the stages at which you will summarize the main points and assess the trainees' understanding of what they have learned so far.

Don't forget that trainees may need help with the basics – how to do simple calculations, help with written and spoken English, and so on. They may also need help and encouragement to learn in order to overcome any fears they may have. In some instances they may even need to learn how to learn.

At this stage you will find it invaluable to prepare a **training plan**. This will help you to organize each training session, provide a structure for you to follow, and act as a memory jogger during the training session.

Timing	Content	Method	Visual aids
10.00	Introduce self and trainees	Pairs exercise	
10.15	Introduction and purpose of topic	Tutor input Question/Answer	OHT 1
10.30	HSWA 1974 S.2	Tutor input	OHT 2 Handout
	Exercise: 'What does this mean to you'	Group work. Spokesperson to report back	

6.2 Timing

A number of decisions must be made with regard to the timing of the training. For example:

- total length of time to be given to the training;
- duration of each session (for example, three hours);
- frequency of sessions (for example, one session on each of five consecutive days, one day a week for five weeks, etc.).

You may also need to give some thought to how you will cope with the trainees' absence and who will cover for them at work.

6.3 Facilities and equipment

It is obviously important to make sure that all the equipment is available and in working order. There's little joy in spending weeks in preparing a programme only to discover that a vital piece of equipment isn't working or that another group has planned a course in the same place on the same day.

You will need to check that the following are available and, where appropriate, booked:

■ trainers;
■ trainees;
■ training rooms;
■ training aids such as OHPs, flipcharts, videos, tables, chairs;
■ computers and projectors;
■ appropriate training software and training databases;
■ simulation equipment;
■ refreshments.

Activity 53

20 mins

Go back to Activity 47 and look at the objectives that you wrote for the new induction programme for your team.

Taking just one of the objectives, complete the training plan for it below, keeping in mind all you have learned so far.

Timing	Content	Method	Visual aids

7 Drawing up the training plan

You must record your training plan.

The planning part of your course is now complete; all you need to do is to record it.

There is no set way of recording your training plan but you may find the form on the next page a useful way of listing all the details.

Activity 54

S/NVQ D7

This Activity may provide the basis of appropriate evidence for your S/NVQ portfolio. If you are intending to take this course of action, it might be better to write your answers on separate sheets of paper. You may need to use continuation sheets to complete your plan.

Using all the information you have put together during this workbook, use the Training Plan provided to write a training plan for an induction programme for new members of your team.

Training plan			
Course title:			
Intended audience:			
Date:		Time:	
Trainer:		Location:	
Objectives: By the end of the course the trainees will be able to:			
Assessment methods:			
Method of evaluation:			
Timing	Content	Method	Visual aids

Self-assessment 5

15 mins

1   In the workbook you were informed that training objectives should conform to the SMART principle. What does SMART stand for?

_____

_____

_____

2   What are the **four** stages of the learning cycle?

_____

_____

_____

_____

3   Fill in the gaps in the following sentences with appropriate words taken from the list below.

Coaching is a process of developing a _____ trained individual's _____ and abilities through:

a issuing specific _____ tasks, which are _____ on completion;

b continuously _____ and _____ progress;

c holding _____ counselling sessions.

| APPRAISING | EXPERIENCE | PARTIALLY | REGULAR |
| ASSESSED | MONITORING | PLANNED | |

4   Complete the following sentences with suitable words.

a The objectives of training should be defined in terms of the desired improved work _____ of trainees.

b Training methods will need to be chosen bearing in mind:
   ■ the _____ of the trainees;
   ■ the demands of the _____;
   ■ the _____ of the budget;
   ■ the _____ available.

c Planning training effectively means getting the _____ right.

Answers to these questions can be found on pages 136–7.

8 Summary

■ The ultimate purpose of all work-related training is to **improve work effectiveness**.

■ Objectives should describe both **performance** and **standards**.

■ Objectives should be **SMART**:

S pecific
M easurable
A chievable
R elevant
T ime bound

■ People **learn better** when they:

■ can **relate** what they are learning to something they already know and understand;
■ are **interested** in the topic being taught;
■ **take part actively** in the learning process, rather than simply listening or watching passively;
■ **discover information for themselves**, rather than being presented with it;
■ **respond actively** to what is being learned and are given **frequent and prompt reinforcement** to their responses;
■ are told the **governing principles** behind what they are learning;
■ are given **frequent summaries**;
■ are allowed to **learn at their own pace**;
■ are **motivated** to learn;
■ are allowed to learn in their **preferred learning style**.

■ Both **on-the-job** and **off-the-job** training have advantages and disadvantages.

■ Training **methods** available include:

■ demonstrations;
■ coaching;
■ talks and discussions;
■ films and videos;
■ mentoring;
■ open learning;
■ computer-based training;
■ interactive video.

Performance checks

▣ 1 Quick quiz

Question 1   What are the **four** key areas of most managerial roles?

Question 2   What are some of the forms and sources of job-related information that you might access?

Question 3   What are the key questions to ask in relation to job activities or tasks?

Question 4   What factors do you need to consider in a PESTLE analysis?

Question 5   What is a SMART objective?

Question 6   Why is support a fundamental resource in planning development?

Question 7   What are the practical uses of a formal development plan?

Question 8   What factors can we take into consideration when identifying development opportunities?

Question 9   How do you evaluate the usefulness of a personal development plan?

Question 10 How will the production of a development or learning log support the personal development planning process?

Jot down the answers to the following questions on planning training.

Question 11 What is the main purpose of work training?

_____

_____

Question 12 List **three** benefits of training to the organization.

_____

_____

_____

Question 13   Training consists of passing on skills and knowledge. It also often involves change. What types of change does it involve?

_____

_____

Question 14   List **two** benefits of training to the individual.

_____

_____

Question 15   What is meant by the performance gap?

_____

_____

_____

Question 16   Two of the stages of the training cycle are: Identify the training needs and Implement the plans. Name the other **two**.

_____

_____

Question 17   What is a versatility chart and what will it tell you?

_____

_____

_____

Question 18   Once you know which person has been trained in what tasks, can you be confident that you have identified your work team's training needs? Give a brief reason for your answer.

_____

_____

_____

Question 19   Which organizational documents are most useful when it comes to defining training needs?

_____

_____

Question 20   What terms should the objectives of training be defined in?

_____

_____

_____

Question 21   As well as performance, what else should objectives describe?

_____

_____

Question 22   In what circumstances do people learn better? Can you give **two** points of learning theory?

_____

_____

_____

Question 23   State **two** advantages of training off the job.

_____

_____

Question 24   When managers are deciding on the best method of training, they must weigh up a number of considerations. Name **two** of these considerations.

_____

_____

Question 25   Describe **two** considerations which may affect the timing of training.

_____

_____

Answers to these questions can be found on pages 138–41.

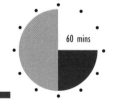

2 Workbook assessment

Christine is in charge of the invoicing department of a medium-sized engineering company. She has been in the job for the past three years. At first she was responsible for the performance of a team of three people, but this has expanded to eight people, because of company growth and expansion.

The job was functional, in that she handled a great deal of the invoicing process herself. This has now changed and now the team members handle the whole invoicing process, while she oversees their work. However, recently there have been a number of mistakes, resulting in customer complaints. Christine is aware that she is not comfortable in actually managing the staff concerned, and often takes over some of the invoicing work herself – otherwise she feels she is not doing enough work. Staff have complained to Christine's line manager that they feel unsupported and that by doing their work herself she seems to be criticizing their capability.

Christine has had a performance review with her manager, and these issues have been raised. She now needs to focus on her development, something that she has not done in the past.

Write down your answers to the following questions.

1 How would you define Christine's key responsibilities as a manager?

2 What skills and knowledge does Christine need to develop?

3 What performance objective(s) would you set and agree with Christine?

4 What forms of development would be appropriate in helping to achieve these objectives?

5 Briefly outline the resources that would support these development activities?

Give the reasons behind your thinking. You can make any assumptions about Christine, her team and her work that seem reasonable.

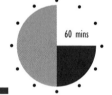

3 Work-based assignment

S/NVQ A2

The time guide for this assignment gives you an approximate idea of how long it is likely to take you to write up your findings. You will find that you need to spend additional time gathering information, perhaps talking to colleagues as well as your manager, and thinking about the assignment.

Your written response to this assignment may form the basis of useful evidence for your S/NVQ portfolio. It will also help you to manage personal learning and development.

Before you can complete this assignment, you will have had to undertake at least **ONE** of the development activities you listed in your personal development plan.

The assignment is designed to help you demonstrate the following.

■ Your ability to take responsibility for meeting your own learning and development needs.
■ Your ability to seek feedback on performance.
■ Your ability to learn from your mistakes.
■ Your ability to change your plans where needed as a result of feedback.
■ Your ability to reflect systematically on your own performance and modify it as a result of undertaking personal development activities.
■ Your ability to develop yourself to meet the demands of changing situations.
■ Your ability to transfer learning from one situation to another.

What you have to do

In this assignment you look at the personal development plan that you developed in the light of having undertaken at least one of the development activities that it contains. The aim is to evaluate the plan and revise it so that it takes account of the development activity you have been involved in.

The first step is to gather together all the relevant information you need to carry out an evaluation and revision of the plan. This will, or may, include:

■ the personal development plan you created in this workbook;
■ copies of the blank PDP form;
■ information about the development activity(s), such as evaluation forms or notes;
■ any material that you have since been able to produce in the course of doing your job, as a result of doing the activity (e.g. presentation or briefing material);
■ information gathered as a result of feedback from colleagues or other relevant people;
■ any other material that seems relevant to your situation (e.g. information about future changes produced by your organization or other professional or public bodies, information about other forms of development activity, etc.).

You may also find it useful to refer to some of the other material you have produced elsewhere in this workbook, such as the PESTLE analysis or feedback forms.

The second step is to arrange a meeting with your line manager, or other relevant person, in order to discuss the plan. They may or may not want or need to see copies of the information you have gathered. The date and time of the meeting will need to be arranged so that all concerned have time to look at the material and assess it beforehand.

The third step is to draw up a written summary of the information you have gathered. Re-read the various documents, and make notes for yourself that assess the following.

- The usefulness or otherwise of the development activity(s) – did it meet your performance objective(s)?
- The response to any material you produced during the course of your work.
- Your colleagues' comments, and any other methods of evaluation used.
- Future plans, in the light of expected changes or new development activities you wish to consider.
- Changes you think are necessary to the PDP (e.g. revising your performance objectives).
- Resources you might need in future.

Next, take all this material to the meeting and discuss it thoroughly with the other person involved. If this is your line manager, only include changes to the PDP that are AGREED between you, that is, those that are approved and have support, and are therefore most likely to happen.

Finally, write up the revised development plan, obtain your line manager's formal approval for it, and keep it where you can easily refer to it again when necessary.

The written summary and revised development plan together need not be more than two or three pages long.

Reflect and review

● I Reflect and review

Now that you have completed your work on *Developing Yourself and Others* let us review the workbook objectives. The first objective was as follows.

- You should be better able to analyse and build a sound picture of your current skills, knowledge and personal attributes, using a range of techniques and approaches.

By examining in depth the actual requirements of your job, you will now better understand what you yourself need in order to do the job well. Each job needs the job holder to possess certain types of skill and knowledge, and to behave appropriately. A detailed personal analysis of the different factors affecting us, now and in the future, can produce a full list of our present weaknesses. When this listing is matched to the requirements of our job we can quickly establish what we need to be able to do.

Ask yourself these questions.

- Do I really know what my job is about, and what I need in order to do the job well?

- Do I recognize my present strengths and weaknesses?

The second objective was as follows.

- You should be better able to undertake a personal training and development needs analysis

By gathering information from different sources, and by using this information in an analytical and practical way, you have begun to determine what you really need by way of development. As things around us change, including your job, you will need to revisit your findings, constantly re-assessing your development needs. You need to regularly ask yourself these questions.

- How is the organization and its operating environment changing?

- How will current changes, internally and externally, impact on my ability to do the job?

- What strengths do I have that will help me weather and manage these changes?

- How can I prioritize and address any identified weaknesses, in order to weather and manage these changes?

The third objective was as follows.

- You should be better able to develop and revise your own personal development plan.

A development plan is a practical means of clarifying what you need to do, while identifying how best to achieve this. Through a thorough exploration of performance requirements, usually with your own line manager, you will produce a detailed plan that will illustrate what needs to be done, the types of development that are useful, as well as details of resources needed and the timescales that are required. Ask yourself these questions.

- Is my development planned?

- is my development plan a working document, something that is an integral part of my working life?

The fourth objective was as follows.

- You should be better able to identify and select appropriate training and development opportunities and any barriers to learning.

As development can take a number of different forms it is very important to be able to identify those opportunities that are directly relevant to your needs. Specifying what you will be able to do once you have undertaken the development activity, can help you decide which forms of development are most useful. You are also now aware that you like to learn in a particular way, i.e. that you have a preferred learning style. This means that certain forms of development will be more appropriate to you and your personal needs, than will others. The key questions are these.

- What are my performance objectives – what will I be able to do, what will I know, once I have completed the development activity?

- How do I learn, and what development opportunities are suitable to my preferred learning style?

- Am I overlooking development opportunities because they don't suit my preferred learning style?

The fifth objective was as follows.

■ You should be better able to evaluate and record the training and development activities that you have been involved in.

Every development plan needs to be revised and amended, so that it remains current and reliable. You revise and amend your plan after evaluating it. This involves considering the effectiveness of the development activities, as well as the direct impact of the development on your performance at work. If your development plan is to be a real working document it needs to change and reflect the realities of your own situation. Evaluation should always involve you in asking these questions.

■ How has the development that I have undertaken improved my performance at work?

■ What do I do and/or know now that I did not do and/or know before the development took place?

■ Was this the most appropriate form of development for my particular situation or need?

The sixth objective was as follows.

■ Use different techniques to collect and analyse information for training needs analysis purposes.

Within the workbook we have introduced you to a number of techniques that can be used to collect and analyse the type of information you require for this purpose. We introduced you to job analysis techniques using job descriptions, talking to people and observing them. We looked at task analysis, which requires a more detailed study of the knowledge and skill demands of a task. We also studied the use of versatility charts, diff-rating scales and appraisal interviews. This range of techniques will give you a sufficiently broad sample to select from.

You may now need to consider the following.

■ Which of the techniques that you have been introduced to are suitable for use with your work team?

■ Do you possess the necessary skills to carry out these techniques?

The seventh objective was as follows.

■ Contribute to the identification of training and development needs for individuals and work teams.

If you have read this workbook carefully you will be aware that work team training needs are derived from work team objectives – which in turn must originate from the business strategy of the organization. You will also be aware that the manager must consider each member of the work team individually and decide what each member needs to enable him or her to perform better. It is important that the manager play a role in this task.

Some questions to ask yourself here are these.

■ Do you consider this task to be part of your role?

_____

_____

■ How can the identification of training needs be fitted into the work schedule?

_____

_____

■ Should the appraisal interview have a part to play in the process?

_____

_____

The eighth objective was as follows.

■ Set objectives for training and development.

Setting objectives is the first task when planning training as the trainer/manager must decide exactly what they are trying to achieve. Training objectives that are Specific, Measurable, Achievable, Relevant and Time bound will do this. In this workbook we asked you to write some training objectives for an induction programme.

An issue for you to think about here is:

■ How can you ensure that all training programmes have objectives?

The ninth objective was as follows.

■ Contribute to planning training and development.

When training needs are identified someone has to decide the details of how the training needs are to be met. The manager is in a unique position to make a significant contribution to this task. Managers know the work teams or the individuals well, and know what training methods would be most suitable and over what period of time the training should take place. They are also in a position to make recommendations on other issues, such as topics, on-the-job or off-the-job training, types of trainer etc. In this workbook we have introduced you to the issues around the subject of planning training and development.

Some things for you to reflect on about this topic are:

- What role do you think you should play in planning training and development?

- What facilities, equipment and trainers are available to you for training?

- Is there a budget for training?

- What types of training methods do you think would be most suitable for your work team?

The final objective was:

- Draw up a training plan.

In the workbook we explained that once all the planning is done the decisions made need to be recorded. We also suggested how to record the training plan.

Final subjects you could think about are:

- In what format do you want to record your training plans? Should this format be one the whole organization uses or just your department?

- What part do you think you should play in drawing up a training plan?

2 Action plan

Use this plan to further develop for yourself a course of action you want to take. Make a note in the left-hand column of the issues or problems you want to tackle, and then decide what you intend to do, and make a note in column 2.

The resources you need might include time, materials, information or money. You may need to negotiate for some of them, but they could be something easily acquired, like half an hour of somebody's time, or a chapter of a book. Put whatever you need in column 3. No plan means anything without a timescale, so put a realistic target completion date in column 4.

Finally, describe the outcome you want to achieve as a result of this plan, whether it is for your own benefit or advancement, or a more efficient way of doing things.

Desired outcomes				
	1 Issues	2 Action	3 Resources	4 Target completion
Actual outcomes				

3 Extensions

Extension I	Book	*The Manual of Learning Styles*
	Author	Peter Honey and Alan Mumford
	Edition	Revised edition 1992
	Publisher	Peter Honey Publications
	ISBN	095 08444 7 0

Extension 2	Book	*Using Your Learning Styles*
	Author	Peter Honey and Alan Mumford
	Edition	1986
	Publisher	Peter Honey Publications
	ISBN	095 08444 38

Extension 3	Book	*Training Needs Analysis in the Workplace*
	Author	Robyn Peterson
	Edition	1998 (2nd edition)
	Publisher	Kogan Page

Extension 4	Open Learning	*The Trainer Development Programme: a flexible ten-day programme of workshop sessions*
	Author	Leslie Rae
	Edition	1994
	Publisher	Kogan Page

Extension 5	Book	*Creating a Training and Development Strategy*
	Author	Andrew Mayo
	Edition	1998
	Publisher	Chartered Institute of Personnel and Development

Extension 6	Book	*How to Write and Prepare Training Materials*
	Author	Nancy Stimson
	Edition	2002 (2nd edition)
	Publisher	Kogan Page

These extensions can be taken up via your ILM Centre. They will either have them or they will arrange access to them. However, it may be more convenient to check out the materials with your personnel or training people at work – they may well give you access. There are other good reasons for approaching your own people; for example they will become aware of your interest and you can involve them in your development.

4 Answers to self-assessment questions

**Self-assessment 1
on page 21**

1 Job-related information comes in a range of forms and from a variety of SOURCES.

2 Every job is made up of key TASKS and activities.

3 In order to be effective we need a combination of skills, KNOWLEDGE and personal attributes.

4 Weaknesses that MUST be addressed quickly are those that will involve job requirements that are fundamental to the overall day-to-day performance of your job.

5 The factors that comprise a PESTLE analysis are: POLITICAL, ECONOMIC, SOCIAL, TECHNOLOGICAL, LEGAL, ENVIRONMENTAL/ECOLOGICAL.

6 It is essential to seek feedback as others often see us differently to the way we see ourselves.

7 We can make sure that feedback is valid and reliable by making sure it comes from a range of sources; from people who are in a position to offer comment and who are going to be honest and constructive.

**Self-assessment 2
on pages 46–7**

1 **Training** is a planned series of activities with limited objectives that enables the trainees to do something they couldn't do before. **Learning** is how we absorb new information and apply it in practice. **Development** is the process of growth and change that may involve both training and learning.

2 In order to change a weakness into a strength, you need to set yourself clear **performance objectives**.

3 In order to be effective, you need to set yourself performance objectives that are:

■ Specific
■ Measurable
■ Achievable
■ Relevant
■ Time bound

4   **The experiential learning cycle**

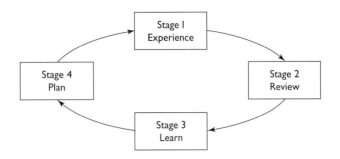

5   The types of development activity you may have mentioned are: training courses and programmes, coaching, mentoring, distance learning, work-based projects, computer-based training, planned or guided reading.

6   You will find a development activity either attractive or unattractive, depending on your **preferred learning style**.

7   The four basic styles of learning are: **activist, reflector, theorist** and **pragmatist**.

Self-assessment 3 on pages 63–4

1   The main items a personal development plan needs to include are:

   ■ a statement of the development need(s);
   ■ the performance objective(s);
   ■ the date by when the objective needs to be achieved;
   ■ the type of development activity and the resources required;
   ■ the method(s) of evaluation;
   ■ the dates of review.

2   In order for any development activity to be effective, you need to **take responsibility** for your own attitude towards it.

3   Factors you need to take into account when selecting development activities are as follows.

   ■ What is the best way of achieving your performance objective?
   ■ Which forms of development are available in practice?
   ■ What is your preferred learning style?
   ■ Is the activity worth what it will cost? (i.e. Is the objective it meets worth paying that amount for?)
   ■ Are there any alternatives?

4   We can evaluate effectiveness of any development that we undertake through personal consideration; by asking others; and by using existing measurement techniques in the workplace.

5   A development, or learning, log enables you to:

■ outline what was involved in the development;
■ define resources used;
■ specify the outcomes, e.g. what can I do differently/better as a result of the activity;
■ consider the effectiveness of the development activity overall;
■ note the time spent on the activity itself.

6   A development log describes what happened in practice, while a development plan describes what we want to happen.

Self-assessment 4 on pages 98

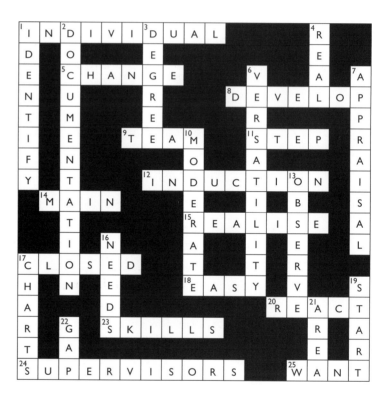

Self-assessment 5 on pages 119

1   SMART stands for Specific, Measurable, Achievable, Relevant and Time bound.

2   The four stages of the learning cycle are:

Stage 1 – Experience a learning activity;
Stage 2 – Review the learning experience;
Stage 3 – Draw conclusions from the learning experience;
Stage 4 – Plan the next steps.

3   Coaching is a process of developing a PARTIALLY trained individual's EXPERIENCE and abilities through:

a issuing specific, PLANNED tasks, which are ASSESSED on completion;
b continuously MONITORING and APPRAISING progress;
c holding REGULAR counselling sessions.

4 a The objectives of training should be defined in terms of the desired improved work PERFORMANCE of trainees.

b Training methods will need to be chosen bearing in mind:
- the NEEDS of the trainees;
- the demands of the TASK;
- the CONSTRAINTS of the budget;
- the RESOURCES available.

c Planning well means getting the DETAIL right.

5 Answers to activity

**Activity 41
on page 90**

Task	d
Wages	0 (−3)
Purchase ledger	1
Sales ledger	0
Stock control	0
Work allocation	1
Control and checking	1
Customer complaints	0
Payment authorization	1
Customer enquiries	1
Data input	0
General admin	0
Word processing	2

Column (d) shows the number of people who require training. The areas for training are as follows.

Purchase ledger	1 person
Work allocation	1 person
Control and checking	1 person
Payment authorization	1 person
Customer enquiries	1 person
Word processing	2 people

6 Answers to the quick quiz

Answer 1 Managing activities and quality, managing financial and physical resources, managing people, yourself and relationships and managing communication and information.

Answer 2 Some of the forms and sources of job-related information that you might access are:

- a job description;
- a person specification;
- completed appraisal or performance review forms;
- an organization chart – showing the relationship between your job role and others within the company;
- discussions with your line manager, human resource staff, colleagues or others doing the same job as you to find out more.

Answer 3 The key questions to ask in relation to job activities or tasks are as follows.

- What do I need to be able to do?
- What do I need to know?
- What personal attributes do I need to possess?

Answer 4 The factors you need to consider in a PESTLE analysis are as follows.

- **P**olitical
- **E**conomic
- **S**ocial
- **T**echnological
- **L**egal
- **E**nvironmental/ecological

Answer 5 A SMART objective is one that is:

- **S**pecific
- **M**easurable
- **A**chievable
- **R**elevant
- **T**ime bound.

Answer 6 Support is a fundamental resource in planning development because we might need support to put our learning into practice, or change working practices. Support will also help us to be sure we are developing in the right direction, with a chance of achieving our performance objective.

Answer 7   The practical uses of a formal development plan are:

- setting out development needs;
- listing methods of development;
- setting review and completion dates;
- itemizing the resources needed to fulfil the defined needs.

Answer 8   The factors we take into consideration when identifying development opportunities include:

- the best way(s) of achieving the defined performance objective;
- the development opportunities currently available;
- preferred learning styles;
- a cost-benefit analysis of resources, i.e. looking at the cost of the resources needed in relation to the benefits of achieving the defined performance objective.
- alternative development opportunities, i.e. outside the usually considered development practices.

Answer 9   We evaluate a personal development plan by: personal consideration, by asking others and by employing existing measurement techniques in the workplace.

Answer 10   The development or learning log helps the personal development planning process by using the information gathered from logging to inform the review and amendment of the personal development plan.

Answer 11   The main purpose of work training is to improve the effectiveness of people at work.

Answer 12   The benefits of training to the organization include:

- reducing learning time;
- getting jobs done more safely, efficiently and effectively;
- having a more flexible and efficient workforce, that is better able to cope with change;
- improvement in morale and motivation of employees;
- reducing the number of customer complaints;
- reducing the number of problems with suppliers;
- increased profitability through increased output or reduced costs.

Answer 13   Training often involves changing attitudes.

Answer 14   The benefits of training to the individual include:

- increased job satisfaction;
- improved self-esteem;
- a greater potential for promotion;
- increased opportunities.

Answer 15   The performance gap is the difference between the way things are and the way you'd like things to be. For example between:

- how well the work team is performing and how well you'd like it to perform;
- what work team members know and understand and what they ought to know and understand.

Answer 16   The other two stages of the training cycle are:

- make plans and preparations;
- evaluate and feed back the results.

Answer 17   A versatility chart contains a list of team members and the jobs of the department. It is used to show who is competent to do which jobs.

Answer 18   The answer to this question should be no. The reason for this is that versatility charts don't tell you what the training needs are beyond the normal functions of the work team. They don't allow for the fact that some jobs consist of skills that can be learned quickly by any work team member. Nor do they allow for the range of skills and knowledge some other jobs may require. They also do not give any indication of the degree of expertise reached by the person currently holding the job.

Answer 19   When defining training needs the most useful organizational documents are job descriptions and person specifications.

Answer 20   The objectives of training are defined in terms of the desired work performance of the trainees.

Answer 21   Objectives should describe both performance and standards.

Answer 22   People learn more easily when they:

- can relate the subject matter to something they already know and understand;
- are interested in the subject matter;
- take an active part in the learning process, rather than simply listening and watching passively;
- discover information for themselves rather than being presented with it.

Answer 23   Advantages of training off-the-job are:

- a better chance to concentrate away from distractions of the workplace, such as noise and bustle;
- freedom from interruptions and from having to put effort into work;
- an opportunity to think through the principles behind actions and perhaps to question why the work is done in the way it is.

Answer 24   Managers need to consider the following:

- the needs of the trainees;
- the demands of the task;
- the constraints of the budget and available resources.

Answer 25   The following may affect the timing of training:

- the need for the trainee's absence at work to be covered;
- that all the trainees and the facilities are available at the time you need them;
- when the new knowledge or skills will need to be applied.

7 Certificate

Completion of this certificate by an authorized person shows that you have worked through all the parts of this workbook and satisfactorily completed the assessments. The certificate provides a record of what you have done that may be used for exemptions or as evidence of prior learning against other nationally certificated qualifications.

superseries

Developing Yourself and Others

....

has satisfactorily completed this workbook

Name of signatory ....

Position ....

Signature ....

Date ....

Official stamp

Pergamon
Flexible
Learning

Fifth Edition

superseries

FIFTH EDITION

Workbooks in the series:

Achieving Objectives Through Time Management	978-0-08-046415-2
Building the Team	978-0-08-046412-1
Coaching and Training your Work Team	978-0-08-046418-3
Communicating One-to-One at Work	978-0-08-046438-1
Developing Yourself and Others	978-0-08-046414-5
Effective Meetings for Managers	978-0-08-046439-8
Giving Briefings and Making Presentations in the Workplace	978-0-08-046436-7
Influencing Others at Work	978-0-08-046435-0
Introduction to Leadership	978-0-08-046411-4
Managing Conflict in the Workplace	978-0-08-046416-9
Managing Creativity and Innovation in the Workplace	978-0-08-046441-1
Managing Customer Service	978-0-08-046419-0
Managing Health and Safety at Work	978-0-08-046426-8
Managing Performance	978-0-08-046429-9
Managing Projects	978-0-08-046425-1
Managing Stress in the Workplace	978-0-08-046417-6
Managing the Effective Use of Equipment	978-0-08-046432-9
Managing the Efficient Use of Materials	978-0-08-046431-2
Managing the Employment Relationship	978-0-08-046443-5
Marketing for Managers	978-0-08-046974-4
Motivating to Perform in the Workplace	978-0-08-046413-8
Obtaining Information for Effective Management	978-0-08-046434-3
Organizing and Delegating	978-0-08-046422-0
Planning Change in the Workplace	978-0-08-046444-2
Planning to Work Efficiently	978-0-08-046421-3
Providing Quality to Customers	978-0-08-046420-6
Recruiting, Selecting and Inducting New Staff in the Workplace	978-0-08-046442-8
Solving Problems and Making Decisions	978-0-08-046423-7
Understanding Change in the Workplace	978-0-08-046424-4
Understanding Culture and Ethics in Organizations	978-0-08-046428-2
Understanding Organizations in their Context	978-0-08-046427-5
Understanding the Communication Process in the Workplace	978-0-08-046433-6
Understanding Workplace Information Systems	978-0-08-046440-4
Working with Costs and Budgets	978-0-08-046430-5
Writing for Business	978-0-08-046437-4

For prices and availability please telephone our order helpline   +44 (0) 1865 474010
or email   directorders@elsevier.com